ALPER DERİNBOĞAZ

# GEOSPACES

WITH ESSAY BY GRAHAM HARMAN
& FOREWORD BY LUCA MOLINARI
EDITED BY EMMY BACHARACH

| | |
|---|---|
| WORK BY | ALPER DERİNBOĞAZ |
| EDITOR | EMMY BACHARACH |
| DESIGN | HAZAL ÖZKAYA, CEREN ABAY |
| CREATIVE DIRECTION | FURKAN TEMİR, HAZAL ÖZKAYA |
| TRANSLATION OF ITALIAN TEXT | ANJA VISINI |
| SPECIAL THANKS TO | BAHAR TÜRKAY, DİLEK ÖZTÜRK, BLAINE BROWNELL, EDİPCAN YILDIZ, ENİSE BURCU DERİNBOĞAZ, LAURA PEDATA, LORIS ROSSI, NICOLA CHERUBINI, RANA IRMAK AKSOY, SIMONA FINESSI, SİNAN LOGİE |
| FIRST EDITION | PRINTED IN PRINTCENTER İSTANBUL, TURKEY, JANUARY 2023<br>CERTIFICATE: 46616 |
| SALON ALPER DERİNBOĞAZ | |
| GERMANY | WARSCHAUER PLATZ 11-13, 10245 BERLIN |
| TURKEY | İNÖNÜ 41, GÜMÜŞSUYU, BEYOĞLU, 34437 İSTANBUL |

# CONTENTS

# GEOSPACES

# GEOSPACES

TOPOGRAPHY-ARCH-EARTH

NATURE-ARCH-EARTH

SPACE-ARCH-EARTH

HISTORY-ARCH-EARTH

SCIENCE-ARCH-EARTH

## EARTH SHAPES

MODALITIES OF THE SPONTANEOUS

VILLA TOPOS

OBLIQUE LAND

## ITERATIONS

SCIENCE ISLAND

KUORI

## TRANSITIONS

ECOTONE

PANORAMA

## EVOLUTIONS

FİTAŞ PASSAGE

MUSEUM OF İSTANBUL

## FUTURE HYBRIDS

AUGMENTED STRUCTURES

LEARNING SKY

# FOREWORD

"I was invited to present myself at the police, where I was asked how I, a foreigner, dared to make a similar attempt against the beauty of Lake Geneva. The building was too simple. Where were the ornaments? I was released with a certificate prohibiting the construction of such a simple and therefore ugly building. I went home happy and content."

These words follow the experience of the Austrian architect Adolf Loos, when he designed Villa Karma at the beginning of the last century. Above all, they express the estrangement and sense of unease represented by the comparison between traditional reality and modern design. Although over a hundred years have passed and our metropolises have grown exponentially, there always seems to be a strange sense of inadequacy when a sensitive architect encounters a place where he has to create a new work.

This feeling seems even stronger and more jarring in the Mediterranean world. Here, the fracture between the slow, stratigraphic sedimentation of time in our landscapes and an aggressive contemporaneity that is indifferent to the nature of the place itself, often conveys an irresolvable disparity.

Over the past decades, a conceptual viewpoint has evolved that no longer relies upon a superficial and naïve distinction between nature and modernity, instead viewing the landscape as a complex, artificial construction that must be carefully deciphered in order to seek new relations between project and place.

We find ourselves within a circular condition in which every living being influences the formation of the lands we inhabit. In this context, the architectural project is entrusted with a greater responsibility than merely negotiating relations between resources, sustainability and future habitats. This further sensitivity that is required is evident in the work of a new generation that is both local and international, disenchanted with the neo-capitalist aim of globalisation, whilst conscious of its own cultural role in the contexts within which it operates.

# BY LUCA MOLINARI

The work of Alper Derinboğaz, founder of architectural studio Salon, starts from Istanbul, despite a more complex path leading from Turkey to Los Angeles and back to Europe. With its conscious sense of restlessness and tension, and the constant aim to experiment with form, space and new media, it is a perfect representation of the spirit of this time.

In two of the studio's seminal works, "Modalities of the Spontaneous", an installation created for the Venice Biennale in 2014, and "Augmented Structures", an installation on the facade of Yapı Kredi Cultural Centre in İstanbul, I discovered an original reflection on the role of geography and landscape as generators of form, that shape spaces and experiences, despite their apparent fragility.

In the first case, the work is an attempt to analyse the fluxes and dynamics of the colonisation of urban space in Levent, a financial district in İstanbul, starting from the agricultural traces through to the recent contemporary development. The results of this research generated forms that depict the urban density of the inhabited areas with a dynamic aesthetic quality. The method was an attempt to stress a latent yet existing stratigraphy and speculate on new spatial and design conditions beyond straightforward mapping. The content of the panels, initially placed vertically at the Biennale, burst onto the temporary facade of the Yapı Kredi Cultural Centre, causing collective bewilderment when a kinetic mechanism activated the skin of the building as a dynamic and continuously changing form. This hypnotic flow of shapes and colours dematerialised the silhouette of the structure, which soon became one with the swarming of the crowd that populates the heart of the Turkish metropolis. Facade, bodies, plaza, gazes, ambiguous forms: all became a continuous landscape, perfectly interpreting the spirit of the city and its restless and fluid essence, which must be decoded in a different manner than in the previous century.

The obsessive reading of geographies and hidden meanings that places bring with them is one of the essential traits in the design methodology of Salon and its lead architect Alper Derinboğaz. Always seeking a meaningful link with the context, they are able to build relationships that do not wear out easily over time. A generational awareness resides in this approach, a sort of disillusionment regarding the optimisation of the modern project. At the same time, they embody a contemporary sensibility with a world that is profoundly changing. In such a fluid, problematic and unstable era, the need to build mature relationships with places is always growing, as the new generation seeks new strategies and ideas to face a time full of challenging questions about our future.

Projects such as the Çinimaçin Museum, the new Museum of İstanbul or Villa Topos seek to ensure, on different scales, a strong and almost intimate relationship between the project and site's geography. Curious to arrive at a tectonic language, they attempt to create spatial links with the earth and the many stories each space brings with it. The projects are often located in unresolved landscapes that seek a responsibility of synthesis. Without claiming a conclusive response, the new intervention has the capacity to activate unprecedented relationships between communities, landscapes and experiences.

Despite the different scales of these three projects, as well as others conceived in recent years, the works of Salon always try to imagine architecture not as an isolated, inserted body, separated from the earth, but rather as fragments of a present landscape with the capacity to incorporate richness of complexities . For this reason, the imagined forms surpass simple formal boundaries. The facades tend to be reduced to a minimum and almost disappear, to open the flow and dialogue with atmospheric conditions: the sky, the seasons and natural light. Only in these contested and deliberately imperfect circumstances can we find those elements that could lead us into a new era. Entering it without having all the keys yet is one of the most important and intriguing challenges of contemporary architecture.

# GEOSPACES

"Species Man does not make history. Man plus Tool does not make history. That is the story of History human exceptionalists tell. That History must give way to geostories..."

Donna Haraway, *"Staying with the Trouble: Making Kin in the Chthulucene"*, 2016

Human history is a tiny fraction of the history of earth. The earth is 4.543 billion years old, our existence the blink of an eye compared to aeons of geological and biological evolution. Human life is a fragile coincidence of chance conditions, yet we overestimate our own significance, talking of "saving the planet". If we do not find a way to think in continuity, to see ourselves as one with our environment, we are missing an important point. We are part of the earth and it is part of our being. Looking away from the established historical references, can we deepen our approach towards the continuity between humans, nature, and architecture?

The earth carries deep knowledge that informs every aspect of human civilization. Architecture could aim to bring us closer in tune with the earth, rather than separate us from it. The climate crisis has forced us to rethink our approach to energy: instead of exploiting finite resources until they expire, we must make the most of available natural sources. Likewise, an architecture more in tune with earth could be one that understands how to exist together with the elements rather than shutting them out.

Our established conception of architecture is rooted in the Classical. Based on a hierarchy between nature and humans, it is defined by plinth, column and roof. Modernism, while claiming to reinvent space, further reinforced the notion of buildings as stand-alone objects, raised above nature. From Le Corbusier's floating Villa Savoye to humans landing on the moon, the Modern era represented a complete departure from our past existence:
a crisis of connections.

Architecture, within this framework, became a technological device to separate us from our environment in sealed-off boxes. We severed our ties with nature, breaking away from our intertwined existence.

Oversimplification leads us into problems. We tend to think of things as objects in clearly defined categories, although we live in a tangled web of intertwined connections. In reality, we do not create spaces but we modify them. This could mean through deeper connections with topography, geology, genetics, ecologies, and natural formations in general. Geospaces is a manifestation for creating spaces in continuity with earth.

# Human Existence is 0,00004% of the History of Earth

GEO CHRONOLOGIC NAVIGATION

What can we learn from a chronology of the Earth read through geological formation and biological evolution of species? The Earth has come into existence as a result of 4.5 billion years of stratification. Humans and everything human-made emerged during a tiny fraction in this huge span of time.

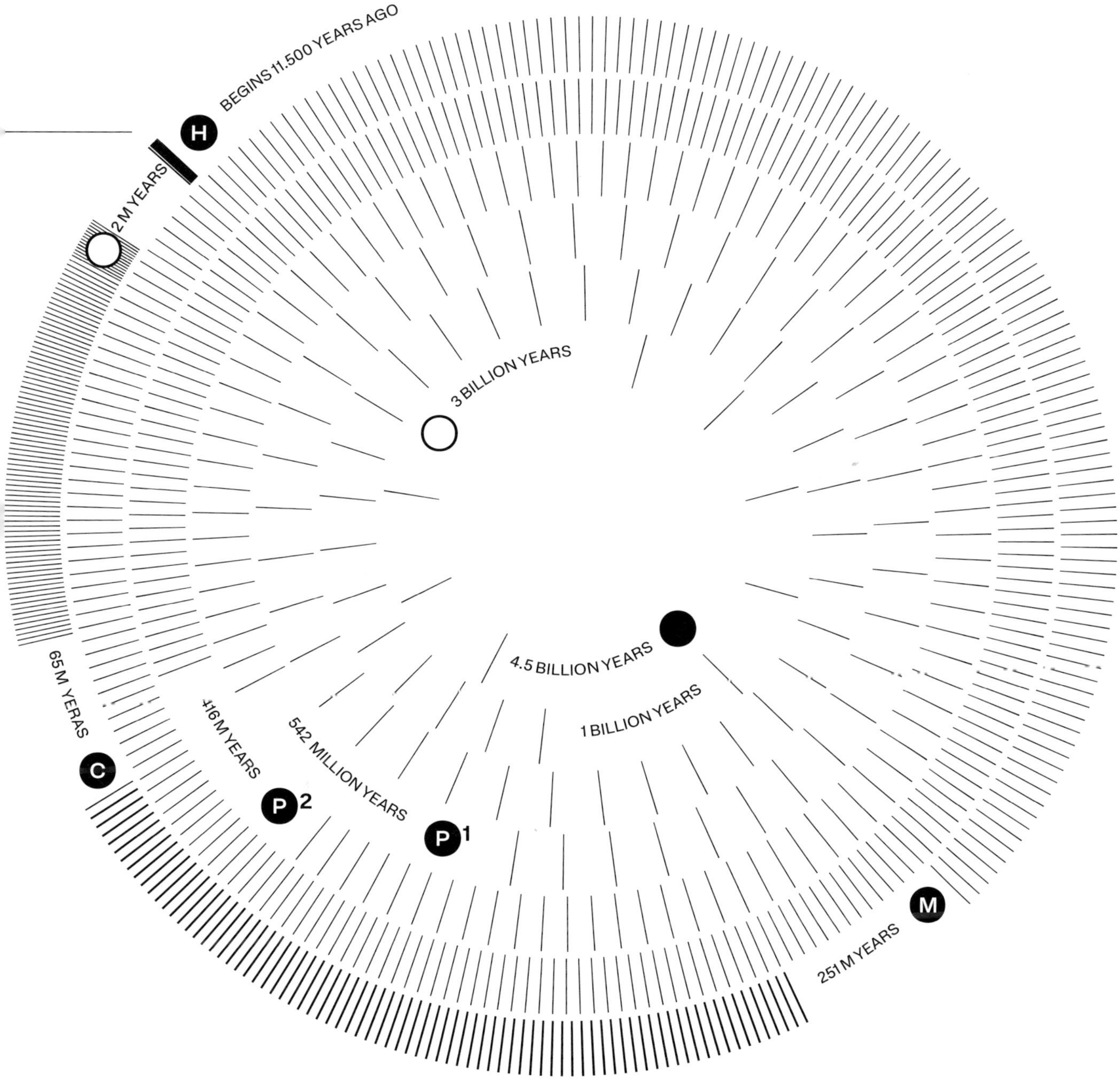


- (4,5 BILLION YEARS AGO) Formation of planet Earth
- (3 BILLION YEARS AGO) Earliest organic structures
- P1 PRECAMBRIAN
- P2 PALEOZOIC ERA
- M MESOZOIC ERA
- C CENOZOIC ERA
- (2 MILLION YEARS AGO) Earliest Humans
- H HOLOCENE EPOCH

# The inhabited caves four that huma of natura

(G)01
Igloo

(G)02
Caves at Hasankeyf (Mesopotamia)

cross the world show us have lived in adaptations rms for millenia.

# EARTH

The shape of the lands and the way we inhabit them are at the root of all architectural endeavours. Cities are an evolution of nature rather than a separate entity, their streets and arteries emerge from rivers, valleys and ridges. Settlements evolved influenced by the natural resources available, the characteristics of the land, and the strategic significance of location. Throughout history, geographic features have shaped development. The cradle of civilisation, Mesopotamia, was called "the land between the two rivers"; ("meso" meaning in the middle of, and "potamos" meaning river), defined by its geographic characteristics, a fertile crescent between the Tigris and Euphrates where agriculture could flourish.

Cities are like habitats that keep transforming, adapting and reimagining themselves. They are formed by and in turn contribute to the transformation of the physical and cultural landscape. İstanbul, as an example, is a city defined by its unique geographic characteristics, split in half by the Bosporus strait. Its extreme topography comes with advantages and disadvantages: the urban schematics are defined by steep ridges and hills, which have shaped urban conditions and historic infrastructures over many centuries.

Modernism, with its universal design logic that ignores context relied on the idea of the site as an empty, characterless space. Similarly, the global architectural language of capitalism described by Keller Easterling as "infrastructure space" is a spatial operating system for shaping ubiquitous consumerist cities across the globe. In practicality, site often dictates the form of buildings, whether through available materials and construction methods, structural needs such as soil composition and earthquake risk, or cultural conditions such as the social significance of a particular landscape. The relationship between building and ground furthermore has a climatic aspect, with the potential to reduce carbon emissions through the use of thermal mass, renewable energy sources below ground and reuse of rainwater.

Geospaces aims to reimagine the relationship between building and site by establishing a continuity between topography and architecture. In some cases, this is a deeper investigation into the topographic context and the cultural landscape. In others, it is about the physical relationship between the building and the ground, the geological layers of the site.

# SHAPES

(ES)01
Aerial view of mountains

# The shape of the lands
# and the way we in
# all architectural endeavo

pit them are at the root of

# MODALITIES OF THE SPONTANEOUS

(MS)01
Venice 14th Architecture Biennale

Modalities of the Spontaneous (MS) is a series of reliefs generated through an investigation into the transformation of urban texture in the Levent district in İstanbul. The project was exhibited in the 14th Venice Architecture Biennale as part of the Turkish Pavilion, Places of Memory.

Inspired by the chaotic development of İstanbul, the work dismounts urban fragments of the city, tracing today's notions through the past. A formal study of topography and parcel borders reveals the contemporary distribution of functions in the urban space. An age-old main artery, now transformed into the main business axis, sits on a ridge, creating two slopes with different climatic and social characteristics on either side.

These two sides have evolved into two neighborhoods with different physical and social characteristics. Former agricultural divisions were adopted as the borders of industrialization. The same land ownership patterns led to recent large mixed-use developments, shopping malls and office towers built on the same spots. Extensive studies based on the built environment and infrastructure were realized mostly after the 1950s. Their informal extensions and comparisons between different fragments show further evidence of topography as infrastructure, which was shaped accordingly, as strong actors in the formation of urban space, as well as accompanying socio-economic and political dynamics.

(MS)02

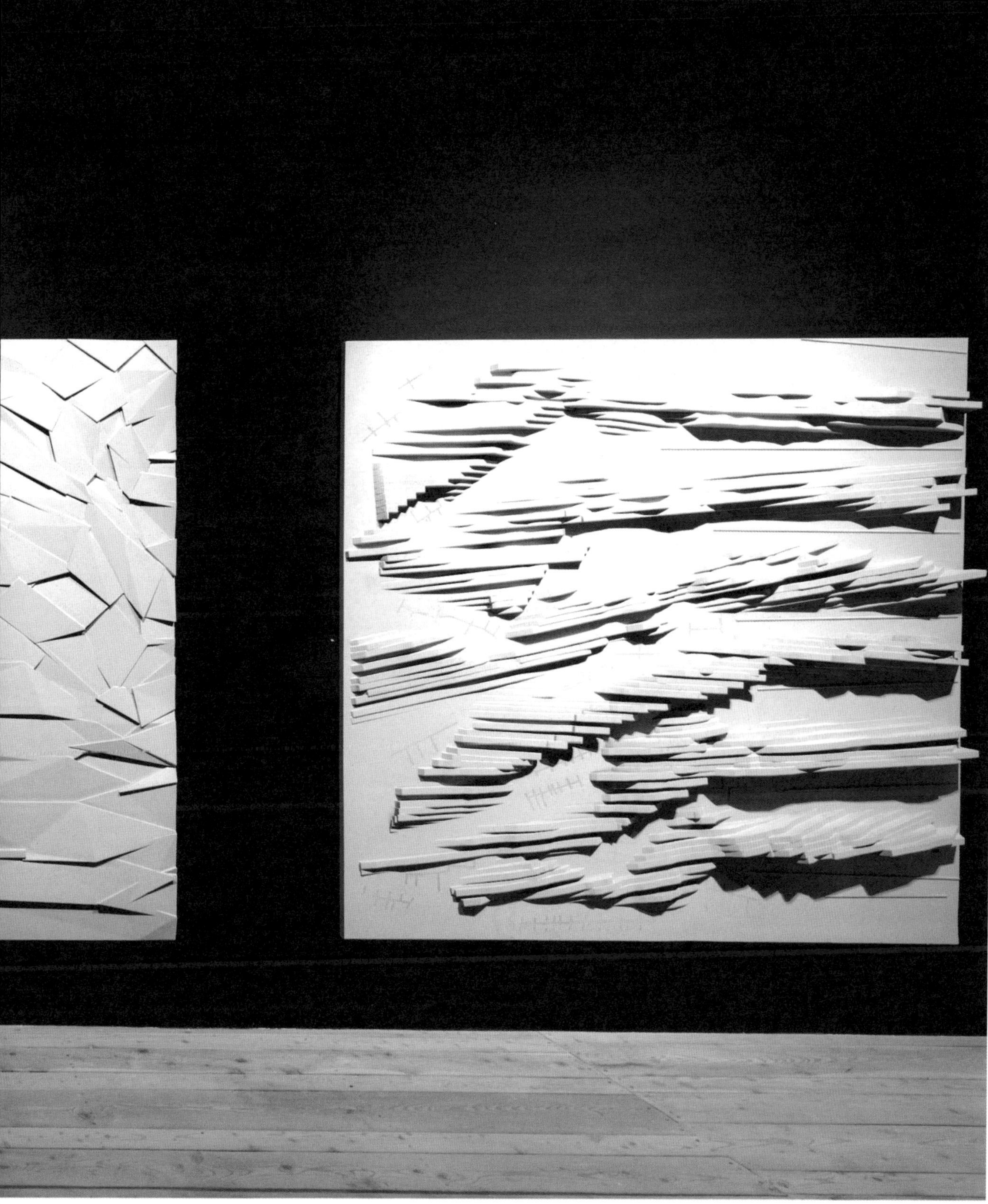

(MS)03
Urban Layers and Ownership Boundaries

(MS)04
A Moment of Spontaneous,
Gültepe Levent Area

(MS)05

(MS)06

TOPOGRAPHY AS AN ACTOR
(UNFOLDING LAYERS)

02

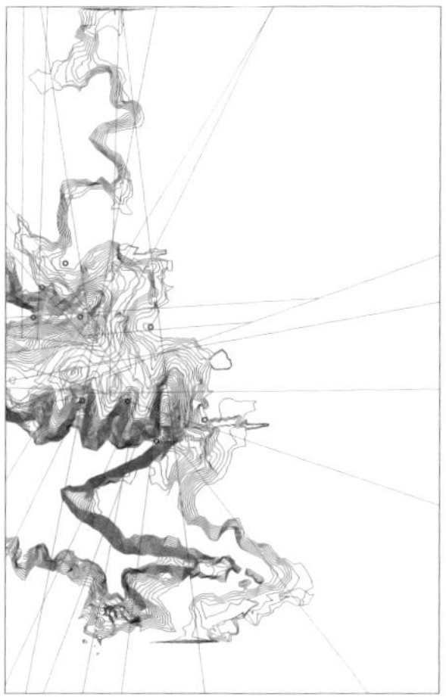

03

01

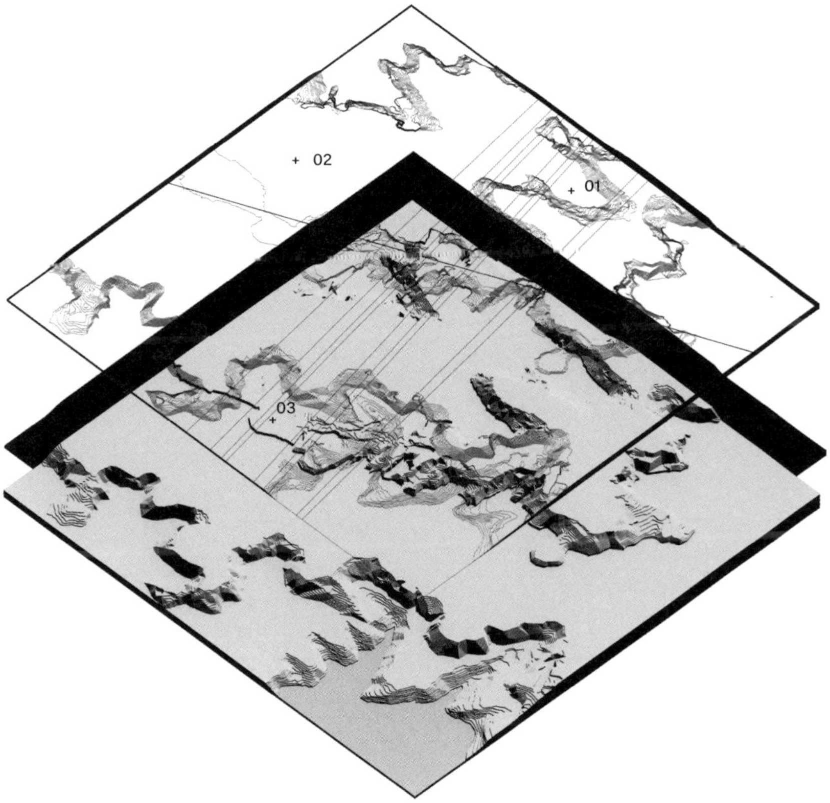


01. LEVENT AREA
02. BÜYÜKDERE BOULEVARD
03. KAĞITHANE AREA

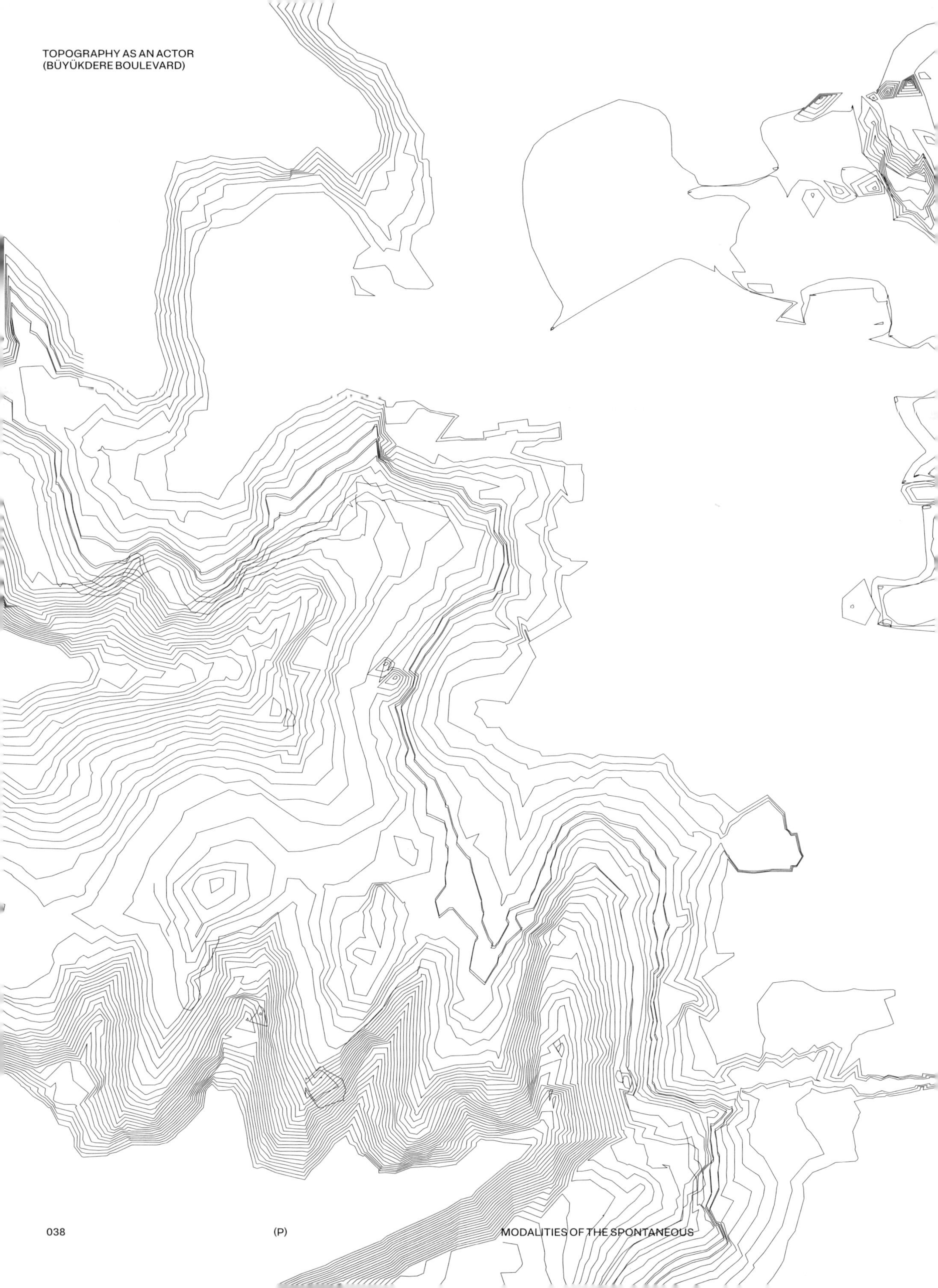

Inspired by the chaotic development of İstanbul, the work dismounts urban fragments of the city, tracing today's notions through the past.

# VILLA TOPOS

(VT)01
Villa Topos draws out the topographic lines of the landscape into its architectural form.

Villa Topos (VT) is a summer house project located on a limestone hill in Paşalimanı Bay in Çesme district of İzmir, Turkey.

The design takes inspiration from the sharp topography of the surroundings, transforming into a simple geometric structure that settles in the landscape. It is buried into the topography to extend the relationship with the earth and to climatise the complete structure with zero emissions. The building develops terraces in the continuation of abstract topography lines in order to multiply the structure-ground encounterings, increase the open areas, and break the western sun to optimise the access.

The building has a unique panorama within the Aegean landscape, far from a flat horizon. As you climb up to the site, the horizon, skyline and landscape of the bay recreates itself in different ways. While placing the staircase at the back of the structure, the aim was to propose a dynamic framing for the view. In this way, the staircase works as a cinematic apparatus that moves vertically, creating uninterrupted views of the bay.

The aim was not only to observe nature, but also to find foundational ways to better engage with it. Wind-catching chimneys create a natural flow of ventilation throughout the building. The thermal mass of the ground provides heat stabilization in the building utilising the constant temperature of the earth. Thus, the temperature difference between night and day is balanced, and the concrete material gives enough time to tolerate these changes.

(VT)02
Terrace staircase

SITE PLAN

The design takes inspiration from the sharp topography of the surroundings, transforming into a simple geometric structure that settles in the landscape.

(VT)03
View from Second Floor Terrace

(VT)04
Staircase

(VT)05

LIFECYCLE OF CARBON EMMISIONS
IN BUILDINGS

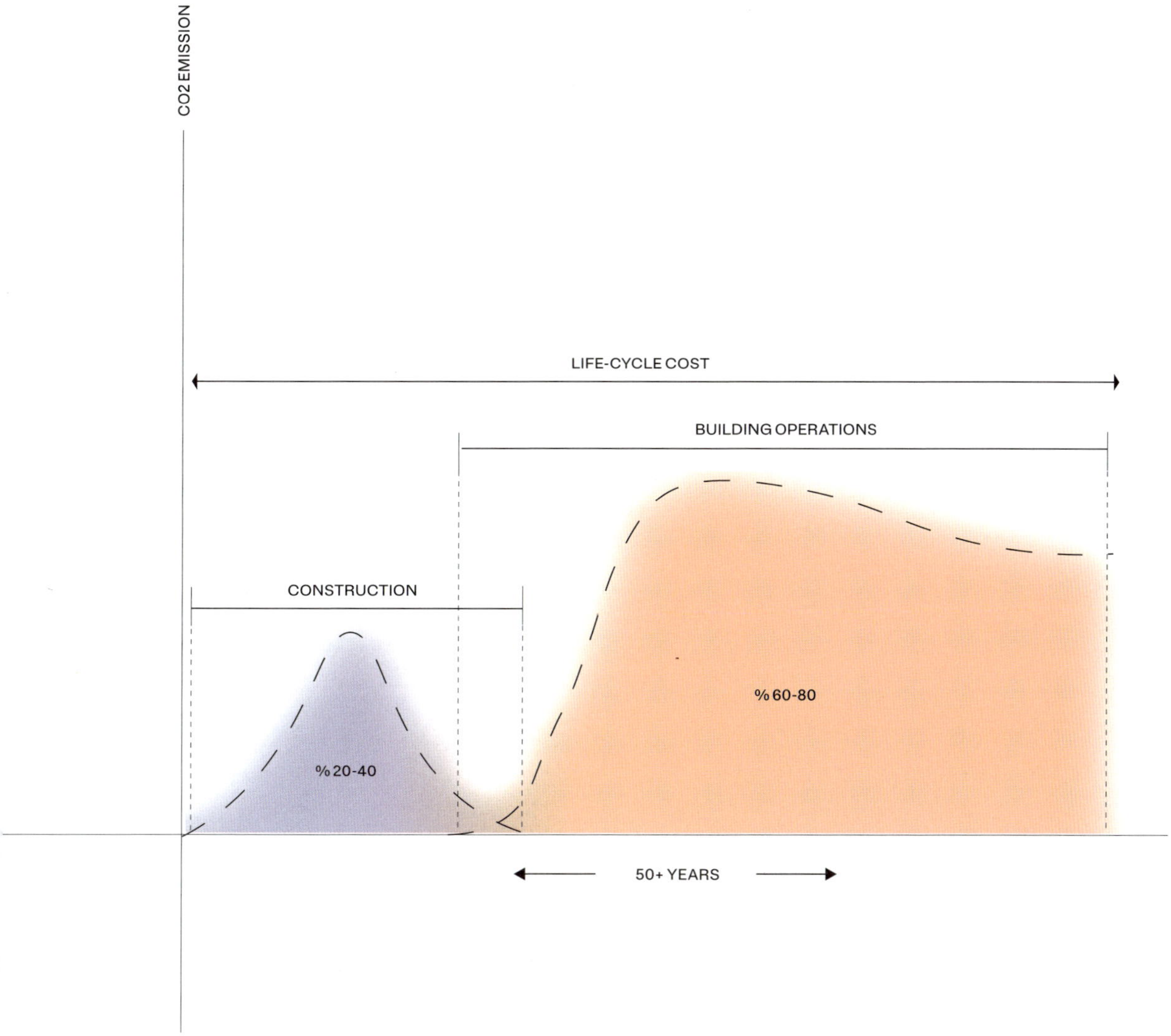

SUSTAINABILITY SECTION

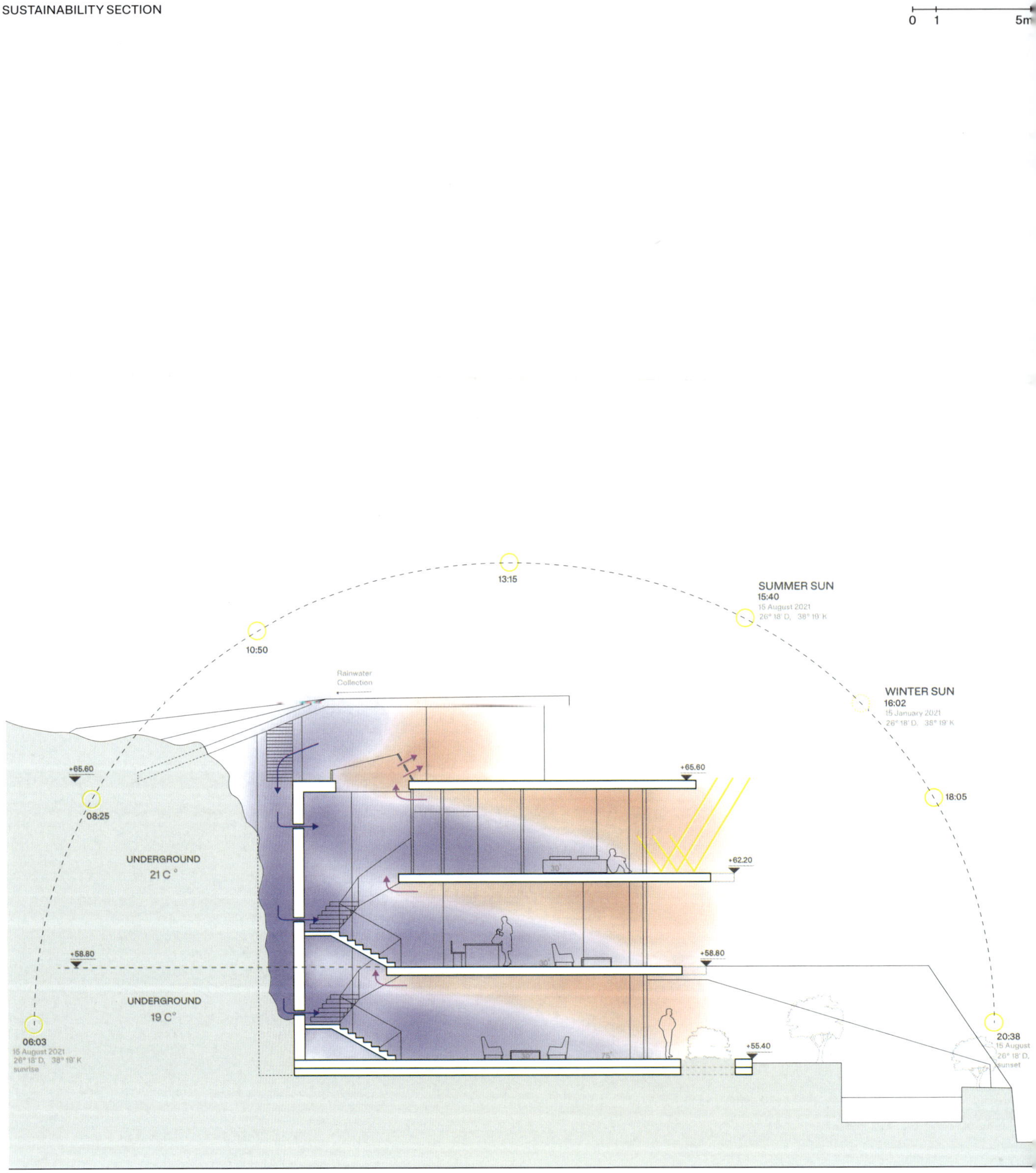

(VT)06

(VT)07
Mass model

FIRST FLOOR PLAN

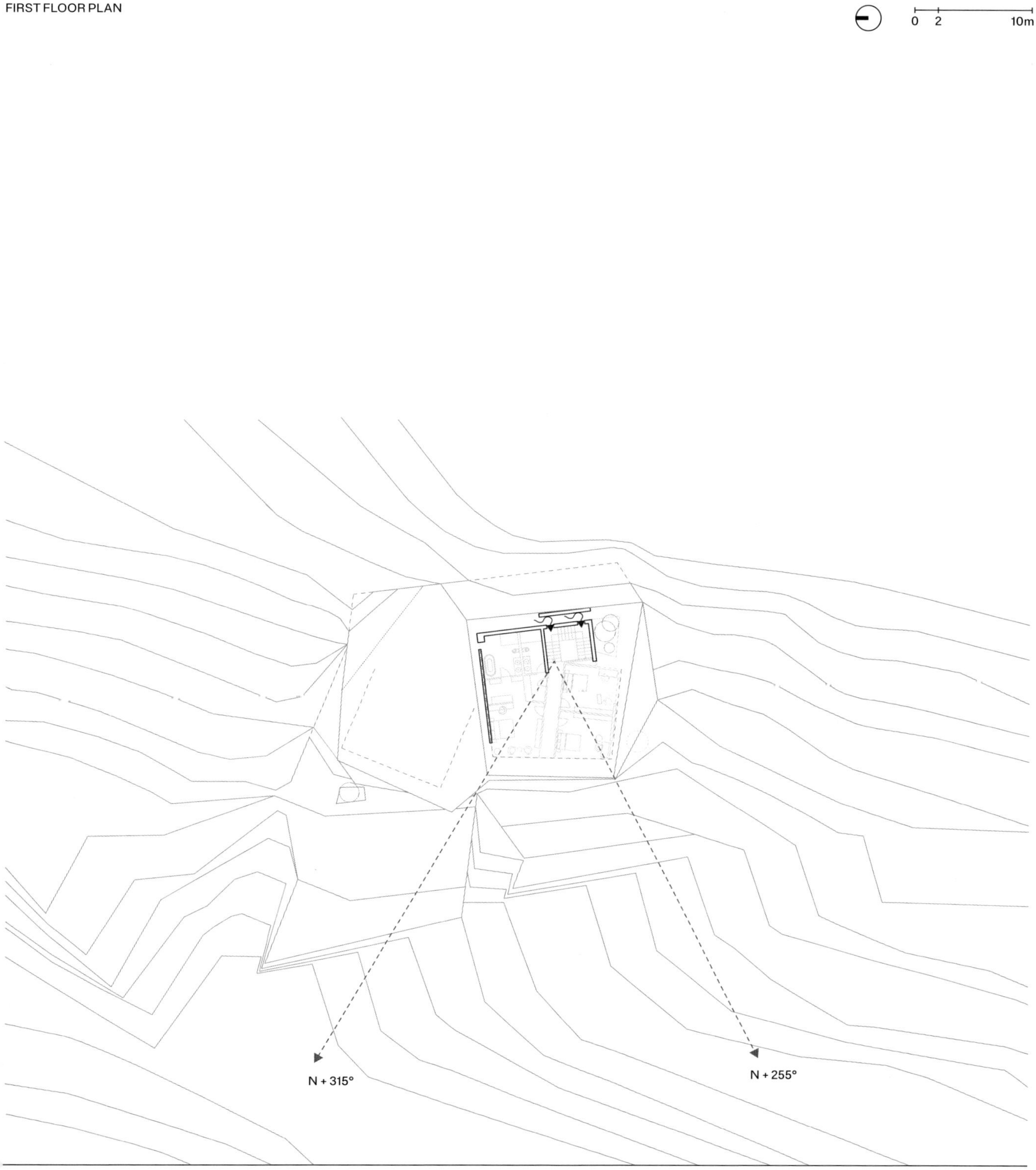


WIND

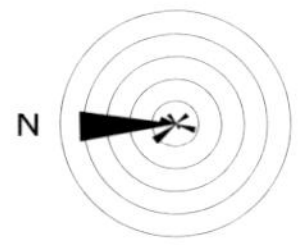

(VT)08

GROUND FLOOR PLAN

0 2 10m

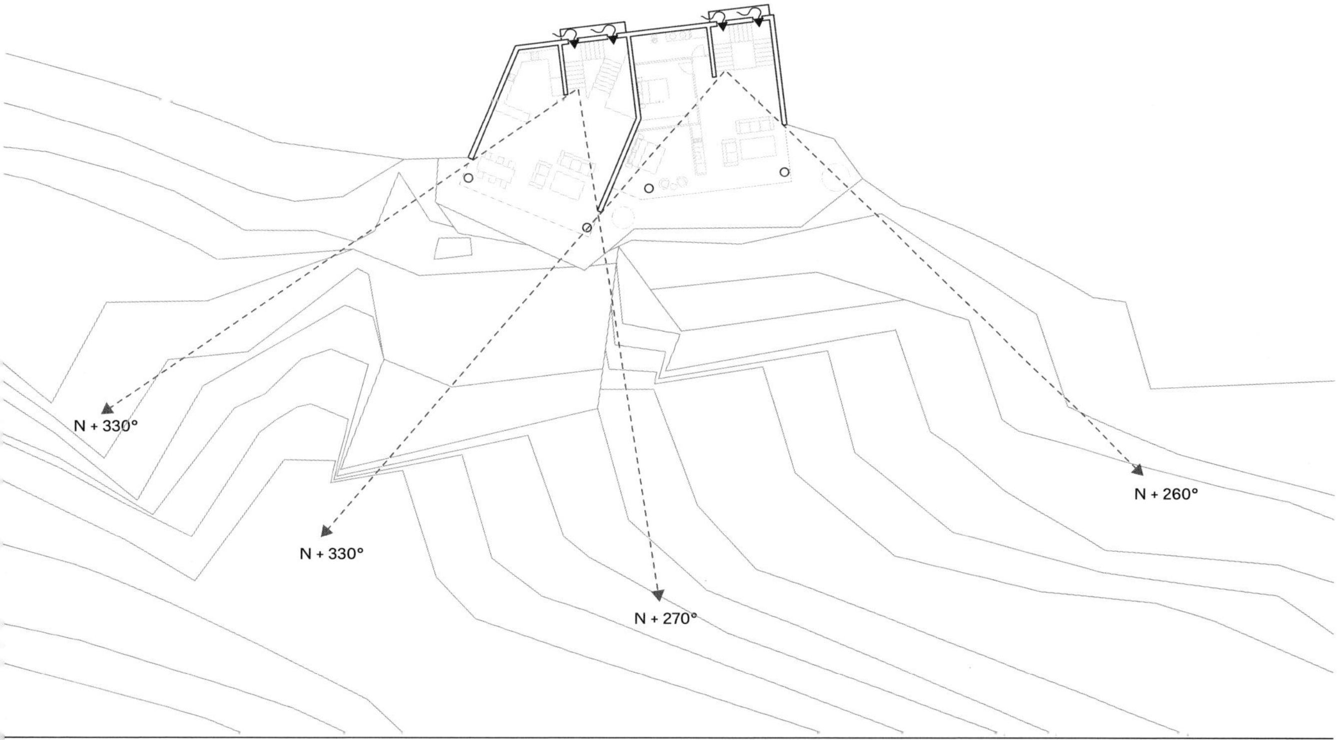


WIND

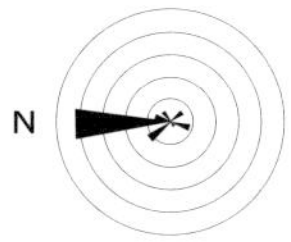

(VT)09

(VT)11

(VT)10

# OBLIQUE LAND

(OL)01

Oblique Land (OL) is a set design project for Jack Throne's theatre adaptation of "Let the Right One In", realised as an architectural production that creates a dynamic space reflecting the narrative, a theatrical topography defined by an oblique relationship to the ground.

The design aims to reinterpret the narrative of the play and to articulate it as a dynamic landscape rather than a background. As we tried to understand the character Ellie's experience of space in the play, we felt that the boundary between the vertical and the horizontal melted into one another as she easily climbed a facade or walked in a landscape. We hoped to create the experience of this intertwined space in a single structure and named it "Oblique Land" as a reference to French architect Claude Parrent's "The Function of the Oblique".

The angled floor is bisected by a pool at the centre, one of the moments that changes the fate of the story, and two large planes rotate around two static hinges. The structure consists of 19 different modules which stand on a mesh structure, reinforced with bolted joints, and can be interconnected and separated from scene to scene according to the specific moments of the play. When the rhythm of the narration changes as a result of the characters' interaction, Oblique Land begins to move and rotate, and the actors play along with this architectural movement. When the three modules of the topography combine, "Oblique Land" progresses smoothly to the apex.

(OL)02

(OL)03

(OL)04
Dynamic landscape, the modular
structure moves with the narrative rhythm

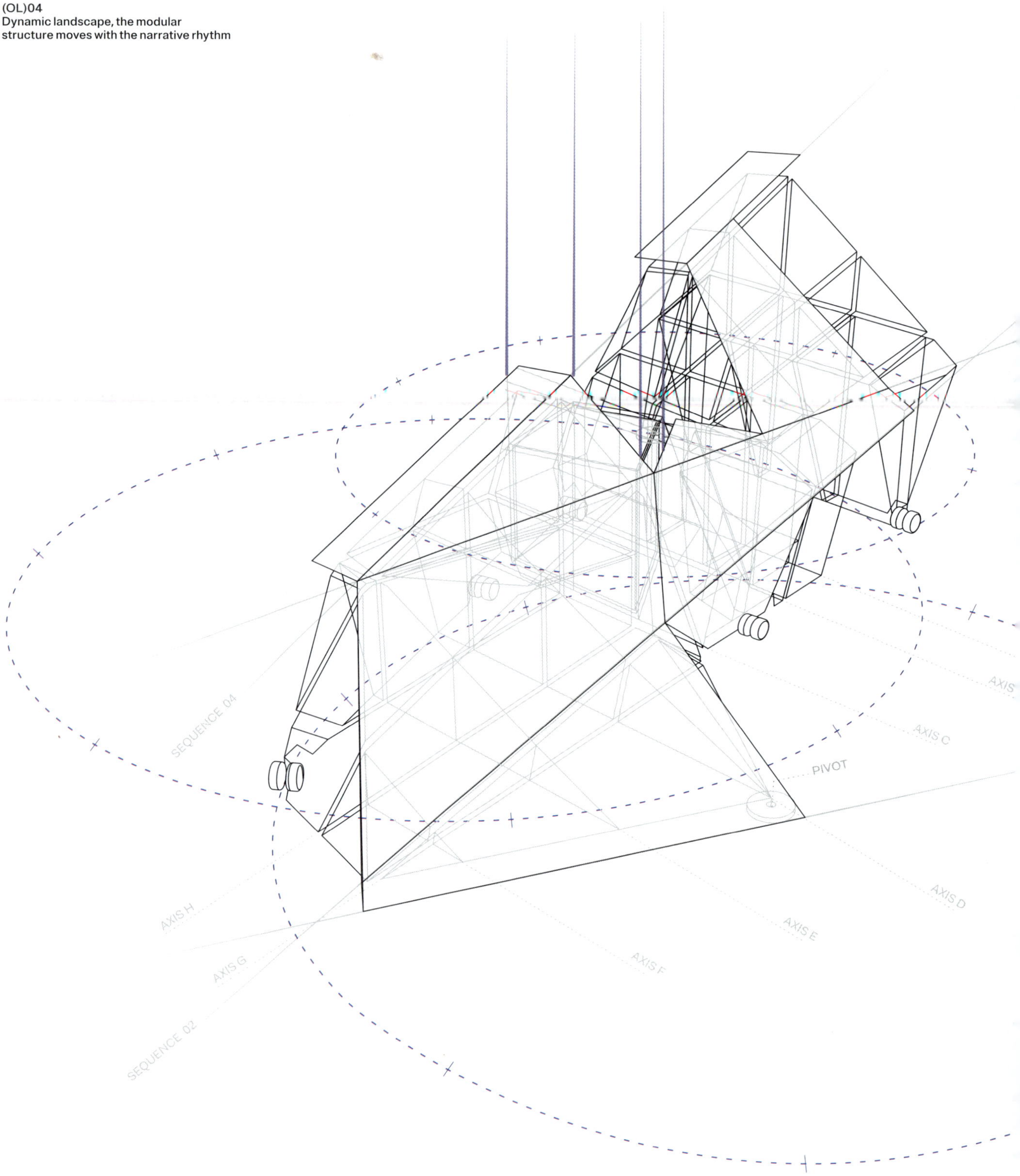

The design aims to reinterpret the narrative, and to articulate it as a dynamic landscape rather than a background.

# ITERATIONS

What if we see architecture as an iteration of nature rather than an artificial object? Through architecture we seek to find foundational ways to rethink the relationship between humans and our environment. Nature is embedded in architectural processes, through form, geometry, material, and function. New forms and species have evolved through adaptation, natural selection and genetic anomalies, so could the same approach apply to architecture? Inspired by Turing's theory of morphogenesis [1], which explains the process of cell generation in terms of experiment group, morphogen and agglomeration, we suggest an understanding of architecture as an evolution of nature.

Architectural history is a fragment of the long evolution inhabitable forms. It is fairly recent that human beings have lived in buildings; we used to, and still do, live in a variety of other spaces: from caves, to mud huts, to tents. The inhabited caves found across the world are one an example of the adaptations of natural forms that humans have lived in for millennia. They present a key reference as iterations, or perhaps anomalies, of nature; not exactly functional in a purpose-built way but habitable in a flexible way. In many cases, more primitive forms of habitation perform better environmentally than their modern counterparts.

We seek to arrive at new architectural forms on the basis of the iteration of natural objects becoming architecture. Form does not follow function but rather function and form find each other. We aim to create new relationships between architecture and nature, allowing forms to evolve through an analysis and understanding of biological and topographical context, developing architectural languages that subvert the idea of the building as a separate object, rather, seeing it as closely intertwined within its natural context.

[1] "It is suggested that a system of chemical substances called morphogens, reacting together and diffusing through a tissue, is adequate to account for the main phenomena of morphogenesis. Such a system, although it may originally be quite homogeneous, may later develop a pattern or structure due to an instability of the homogeneous equilibrium, which is triggered off by random disturbances. Such reaction-diffusion systems are considered in some detail in the case of an isolated ring of cells, a mathematically convenient, though biologically, unusual system."

Alan Turing,
*"The Chemical Basis of Morphogenesis"*, 1952

(I)01
Patterns in gel

(I)02
A photomicrograph depicting ten species of marine radiolarians

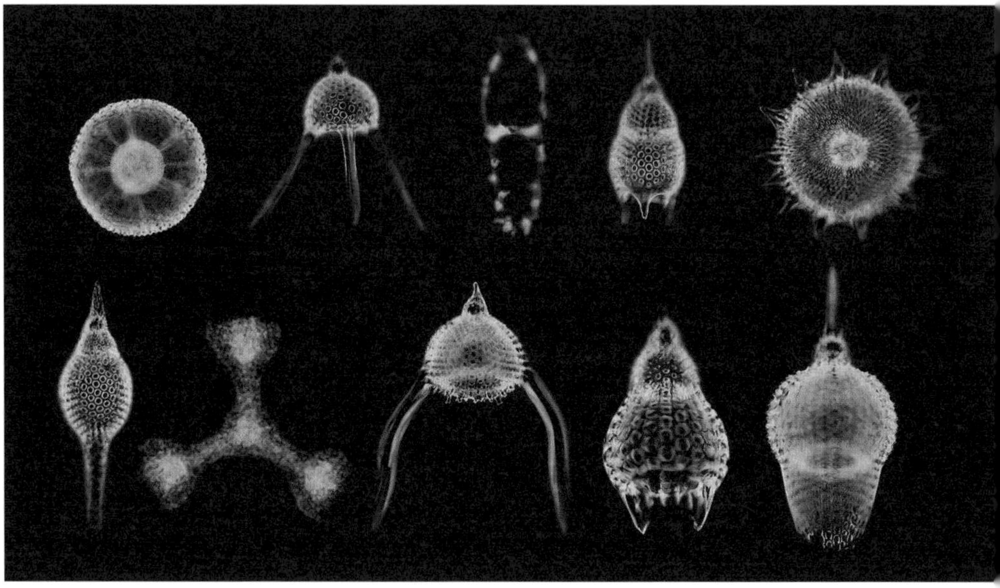

(I)03
Planar Iteration of
Nuruosmaniye Mosque,1748

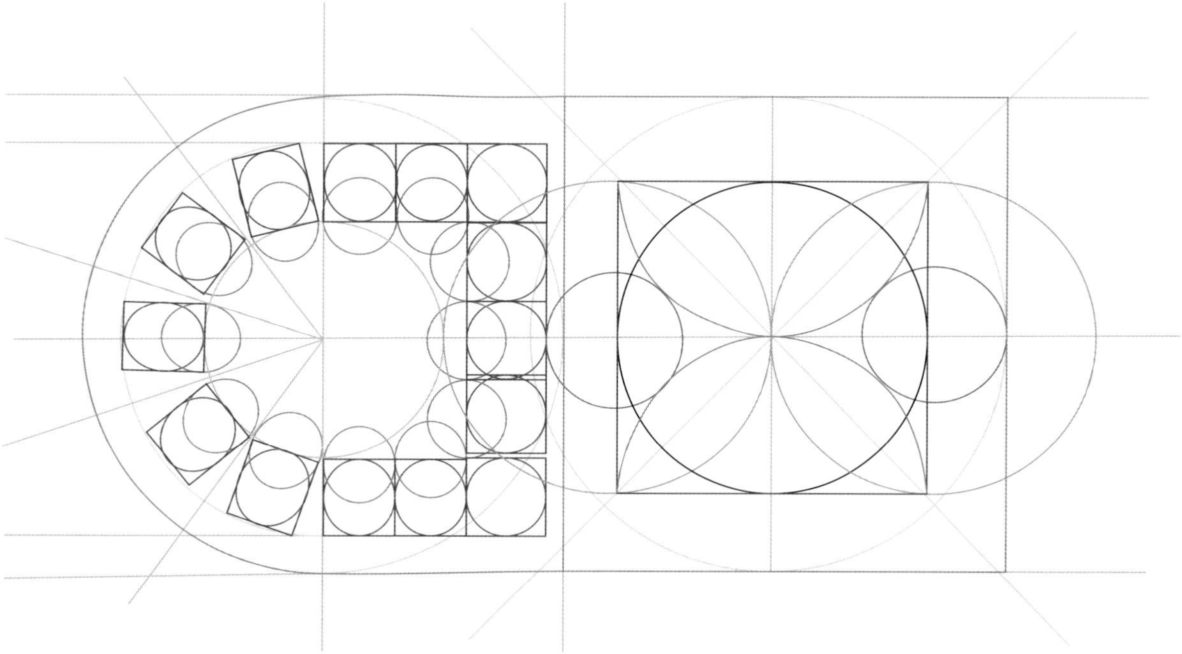

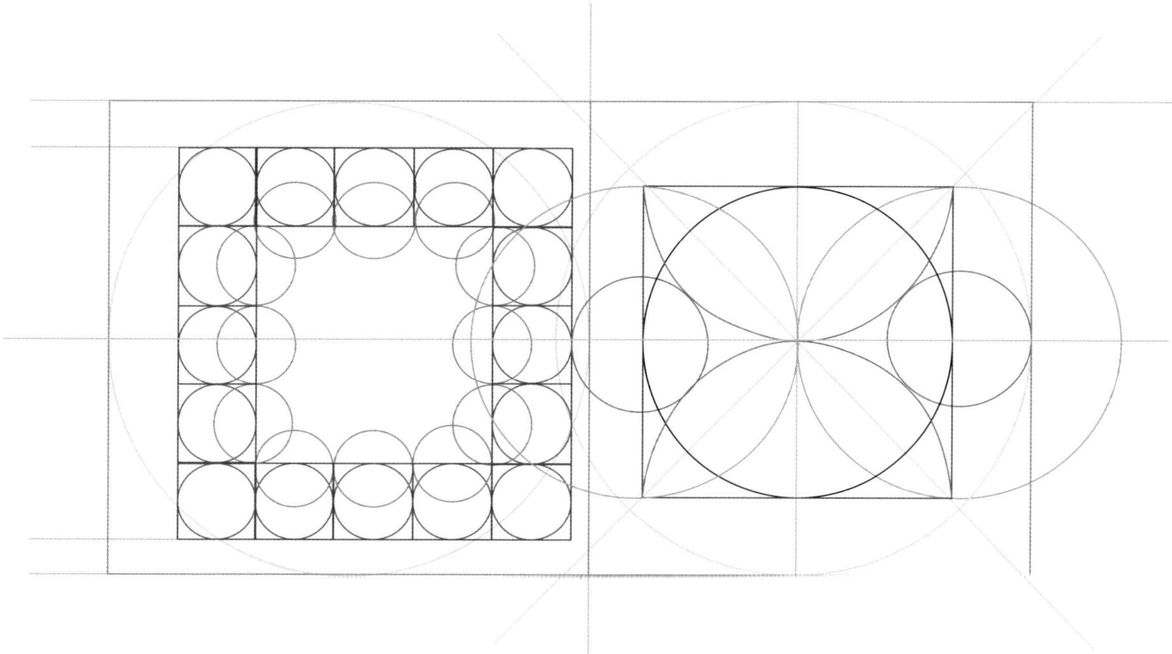

# What if we see architectu
# rather than

(I)04
Cave formations in the Phrygian Valley, Anatolia

as an iteration of nature
an artificial object?

# SCIENCE ISLAND

(SI)01
The design responds to the unique ecological setting and the flora found on the island

Science Island (SI) is conceived as a paradigm between the natural landscape, humankind's intrinsic curiosity about the complexity of our universe, and the responsibility we have within it.

Its aim is to establish a landmark institution for the dissemination of knowledge about our world, and for its architectural syntax to play an active role in the interpretation of that knowledge. The design of the Science Center follows an empathy-based approach to the unique ecology of the site in Kaunas, Lithuania, specifically investigating the arrangement of flora scattered across the island.

The design approach generates dialogues between the old city and the new city, Nemunos Street becomes a bridge connecting the old center. Daukanto Bridge engages Laisves Street. The Concert and Congress centers and Aleksotas are linked with two other bridge connections. A promenade through the Center follows a route along the inner face of its bioclimatic skin, formally generated by architecturally modelling Alan Turing's equation on Morphogenesis. The result is a Stratiform curating a kaleidoscopic visual journey of the Island and the urban silhouette beyond. The clustering of volumes utilizes these visual corridors and maximizes daylight and ventilation potentials within its internal arrangement, a configuration of temporary and permanent exhibition galleries offering immense adaptability.

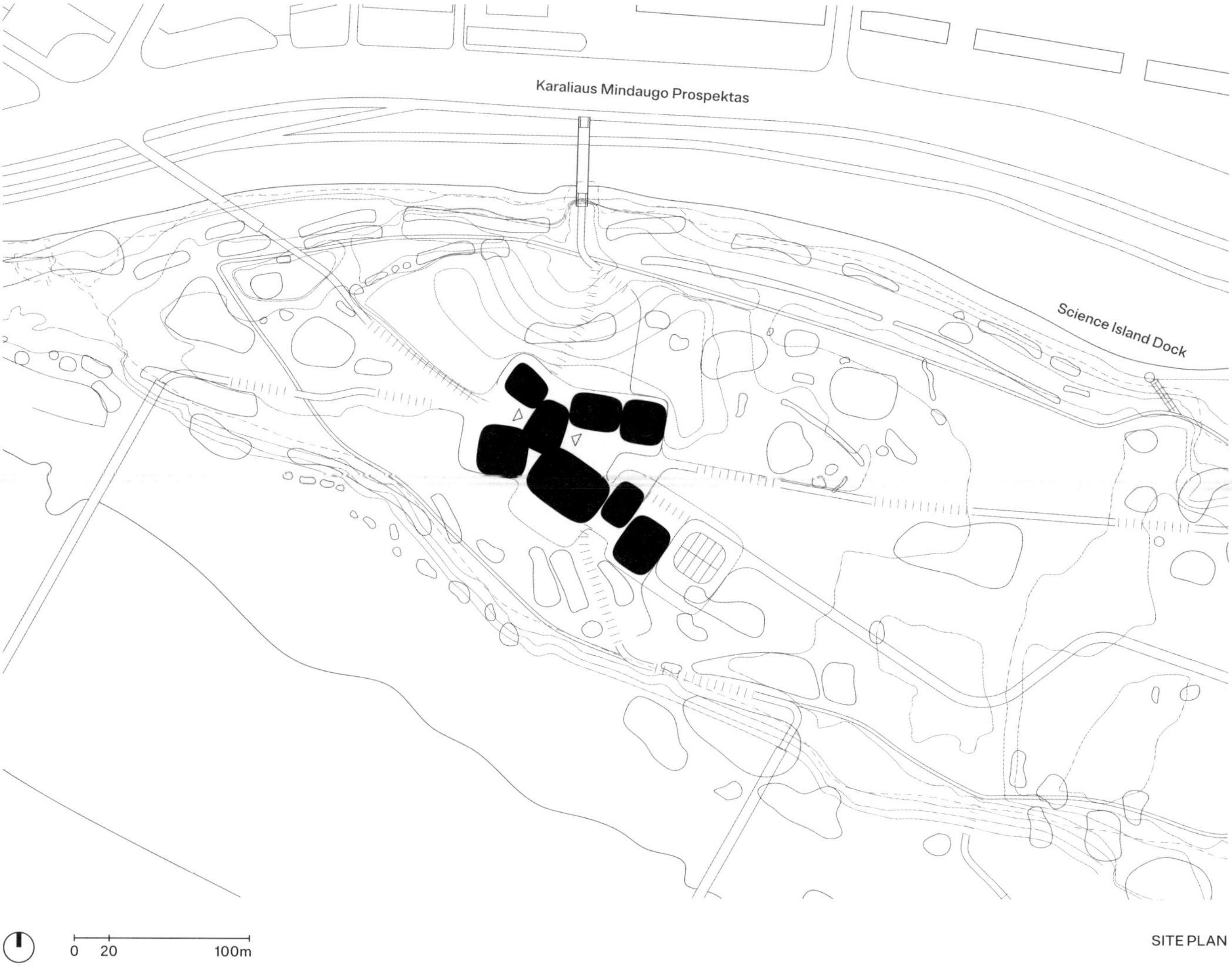
Karaliaus Mindaugo Prospektas
Science Island Dock
0 20 100m

SITE PLAN

Science Island is conceived as a paradigm between the natural landscape, humankind's intrinsic curiosity about the complexity of our universe, and the responsibility we have within it.

(SI)03
Biological and geological skins, generative patterns

(SI)04

(SI)06

(SI)07
A promenade through the Center follows a route along the inner face of its bioclimatic skin

GROUND FLOOR PLAN

01. TEMPORARY GALLERY
02. INTRODUCTORY SPACE
03. INTRODUCTORY GALLERY
04. PERMANENT GALLERY
05. ENTRANCE HALL
06. INFO / RECEPTION
07. FIRST-AID
08. KITCHEN
09. KITCHEN STORAGE
10. WC
11. CAFETERIA
12. TERRACE
13. BLACK BOX
14. CLOAK ROOM
15. TECHNICAL ROOM
16. PLANETARIUM
17. ADMIN OFFICE
18. OFFICE
19. ARCHIVE
20. COPY
21. STAFF & SERVICE ENTRANCE
22. COFFEE / STAFF ROOM
23. IT ROOM
24. CRATE STORAGE
25. DELIVERY / PACKING
26. REFUSE & RECYCLING
27. LOADING BAY
28. SECURITY
29. WINTER GARDEN
30. WONDER GARDEN
31. EXHIBITION GARDEN
32. COURTYARD

The design is formally generated through patterning in size and shape of excisting tree clusters and natural selection of these random spatial mutations.

FORM GENERATION INSPIRED BY
TURINGS MORPHOGENESIS

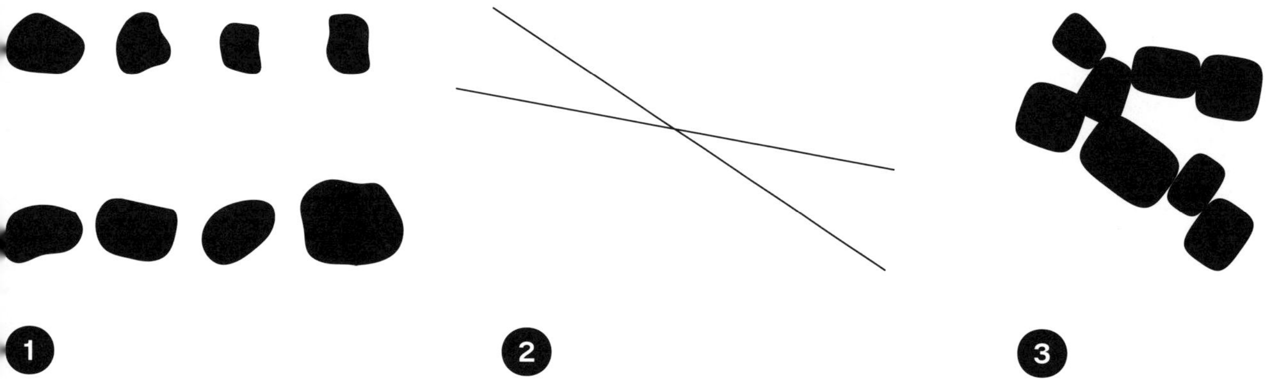


NATURAL SELECTION
SIZE AND SHAPE

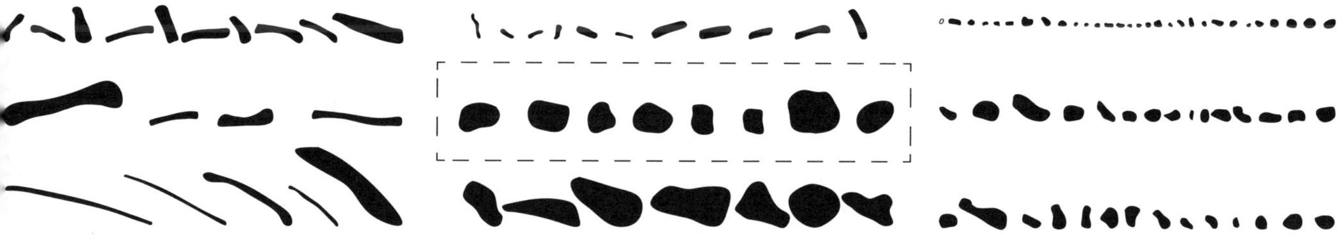

1. EXPERIMENT GROUP
2. MORPHOGEN
3. AGGLOMERATION

# KUORI

(K)01
The timber building forms a permeable boundary between the park and the street, nature and the city

Kuori (K), the Finnish word for bark, gives its name to our proposal for the Sara Hilden Art Museum, the new cultural extension of the City of Tampere in Finland.

The museum is conceived as a Bark that protects the collection, enables its growth, and catalyzes the public life in and around the art. Responding to the industrial heritage of the Finlayson area and the rich natural surroundings of the Wilhelm von Nottbeck park, the museum forms a permeable and living threshold between the city and nature, forming new connections and active public spaces that integrate nature and art. A proposed pedestrian axis forms the heart of the spatial sequence for the museum's open ground floor, a diffused public space connecting inside and outside areas.

The museum reaches upwards to consume light into the galleries through rooftop canopies of north-lights, the gradual expansion of the volumes responding to the scale of the neighbouring buildings and the desire for light. The roofscape recalls the historic Finlayson factory roofs, reflecting the deep-rooted connection between light, craft and industry. The timber shingle facade creates a subtle material dialogue between the reddish shingle cladding, the red brick of the industrial buildings and the natural texture of the tree bark in the park, extending the relationship between the urban and natural context. Timber is used throughout the building, with a composite structure using glulam beams and columns with modular CLT wall and floor panels, in addition to the treated pine shingle cladding and spruce interior finishes.

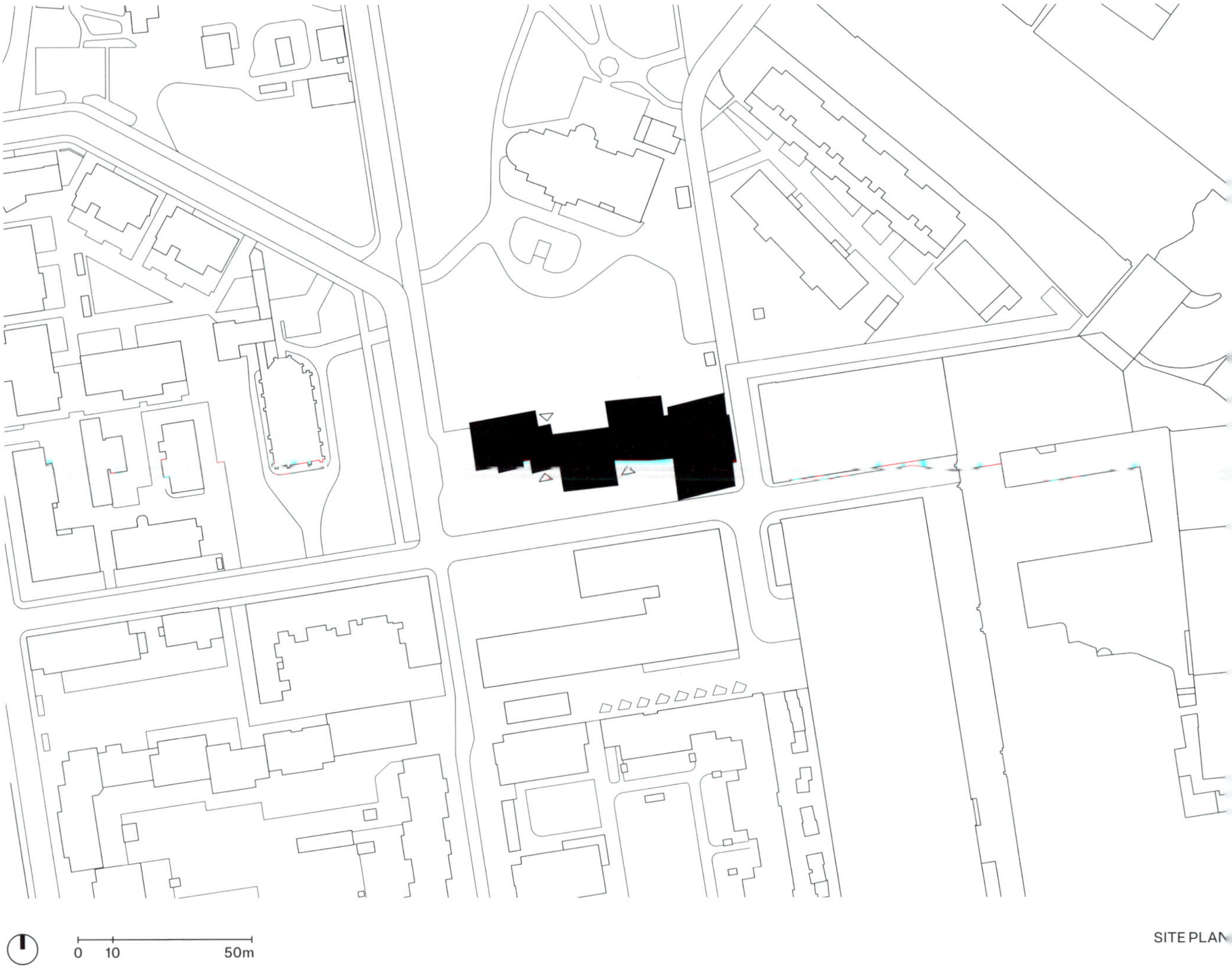


SITE PLAN

The museum is conceived as a Bark that protects the collection, enables its growth, and catalyzes the public life in and around the art.

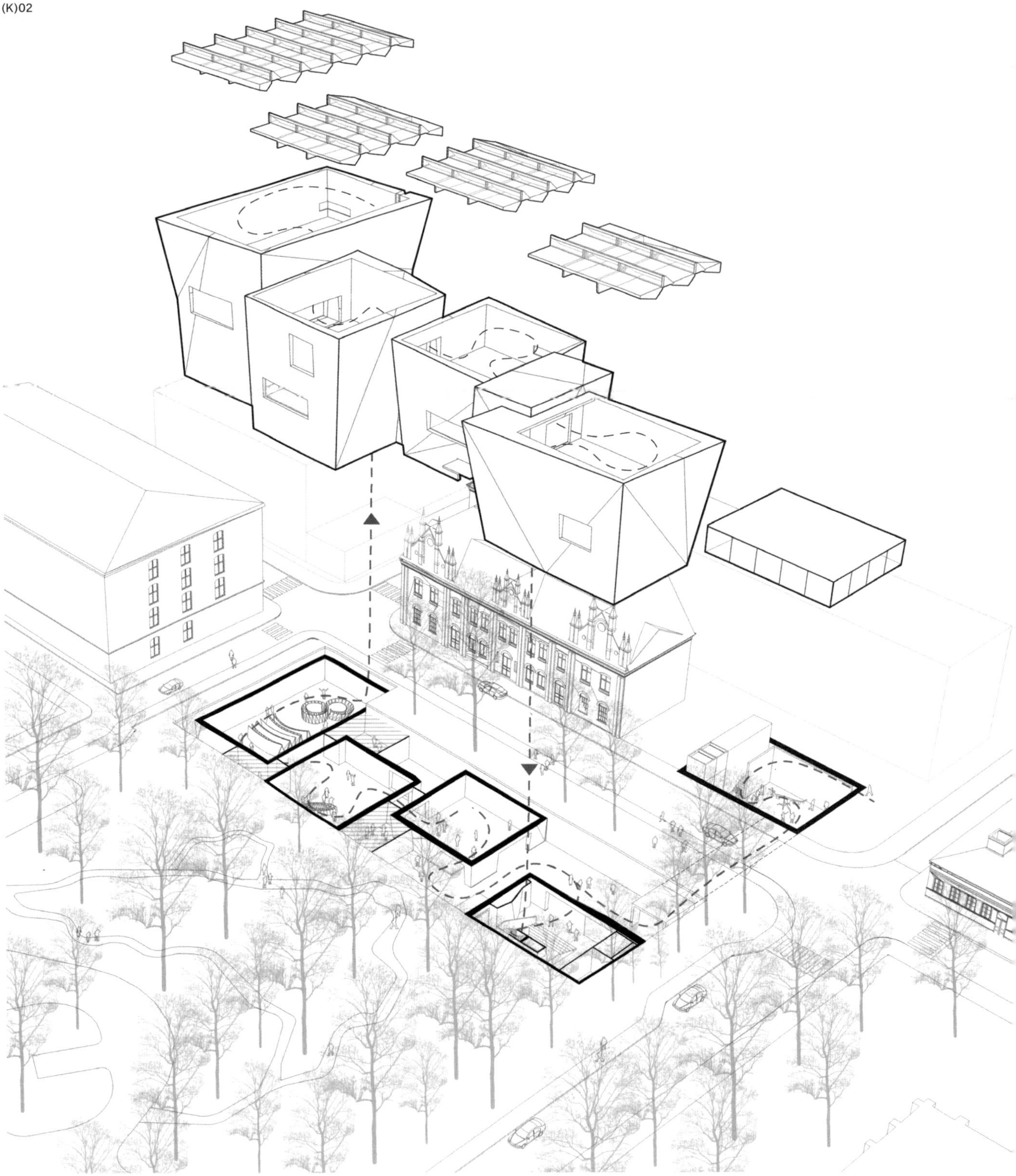

(K)03
The journey through the gallery is driven by a sense of curiosity, with glimpses to different volumes and open courtyards enticing the visitor to explore the art whilst feeling close to nature

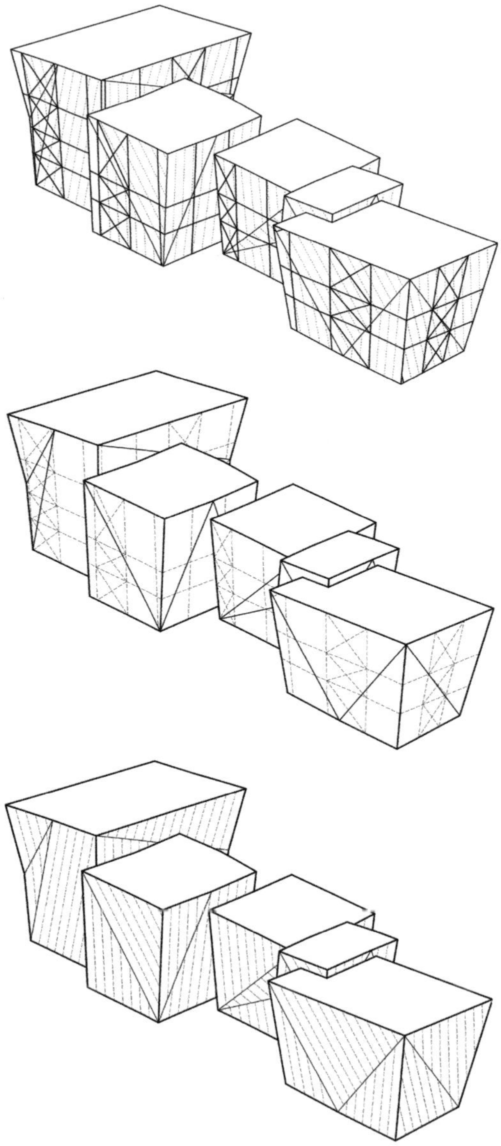

(K)05
The museum reaches upwards
to consume light into the galleries
like a tree growing towards the sunlight

(K)06
The first floor galleries, named a/er the surrounding tree species, give a feeling of wandering through the treetops

GROUND FLOOR PLAN

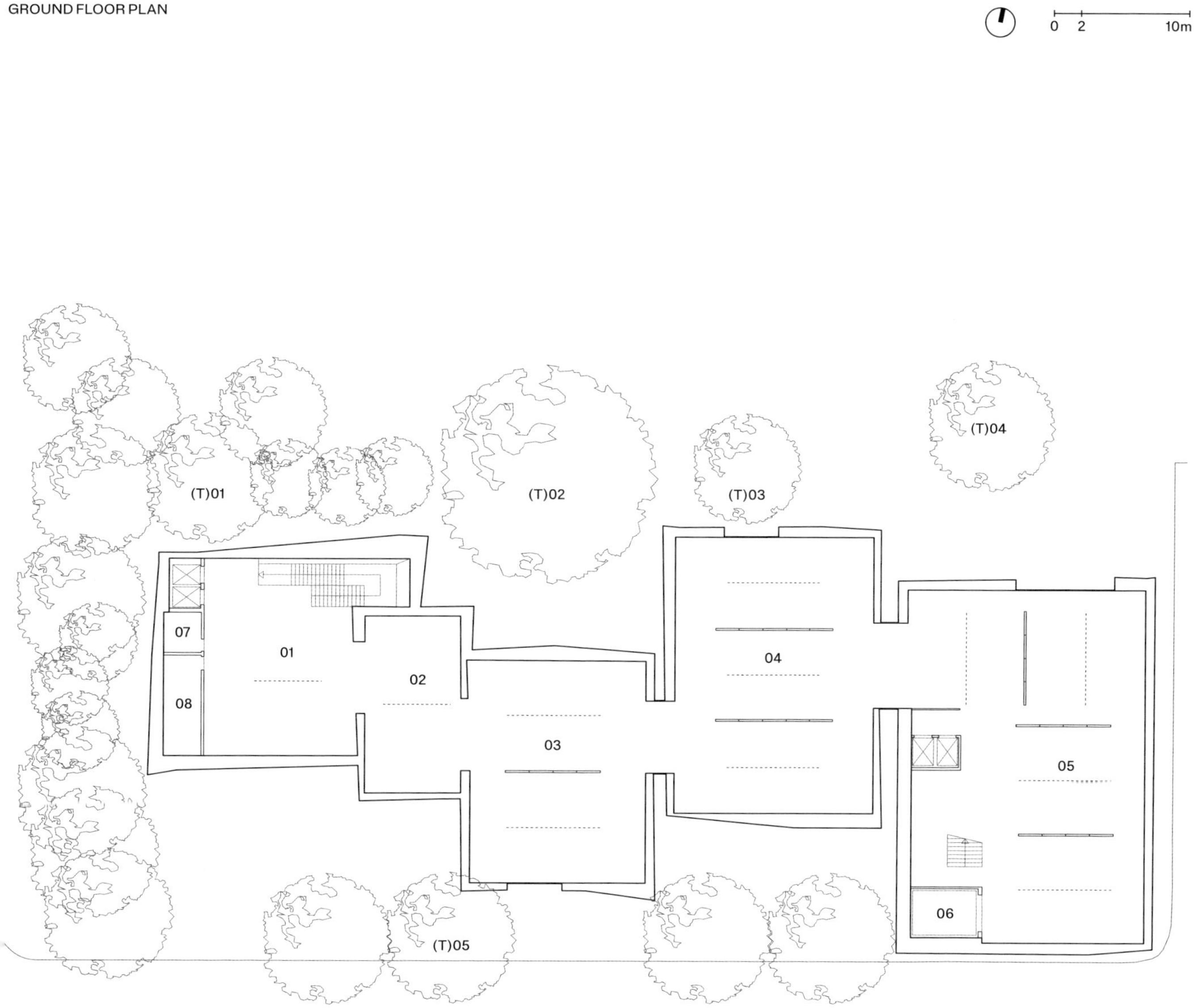


01. JALAVA GALLERY
02. TAMMI GALLERY
03. LEHMUS GALLERY
04. VAAHTER GALLERY
05. LIME GALLERY
06. FREIGHT ELEVATOR
07. CLEANING ROOM
08. STORAGE

SECTION

0 2 10m

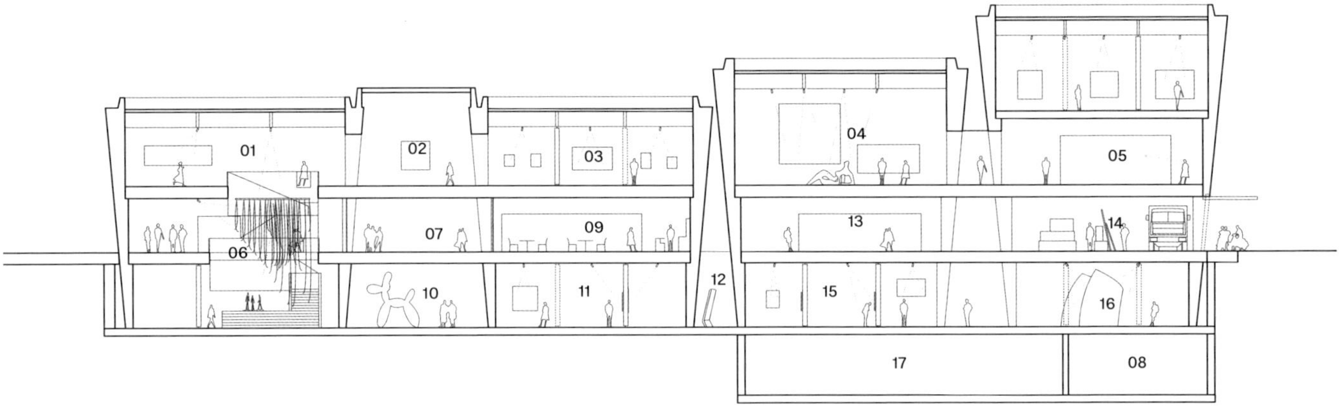


01. JALAVA GALLERY
02. TAMMI GALLERY
03. LEHMUS GALLERY
04. VAAHTER GALLERY
05. LIME GALLERY
06. SARA HILDEN ATRIUM
07. KIMMO KAVIANTOS PASSAGE
08. STORAGE
09. PUISTO CAFE
10. KUORI GALLERY
11. MÄNTY GALLERY
12. LÄHTÖ COURT
13. MULTIFUNCTIONAL SPACE
14. LOADING SPACE
15. KUUSI GALLERY
16. KOIVU GALLERY
17. MECHANICAL & TECHNICAL ROOM
18. SARA HILDENS MUSEUM SQUARE

SECTION

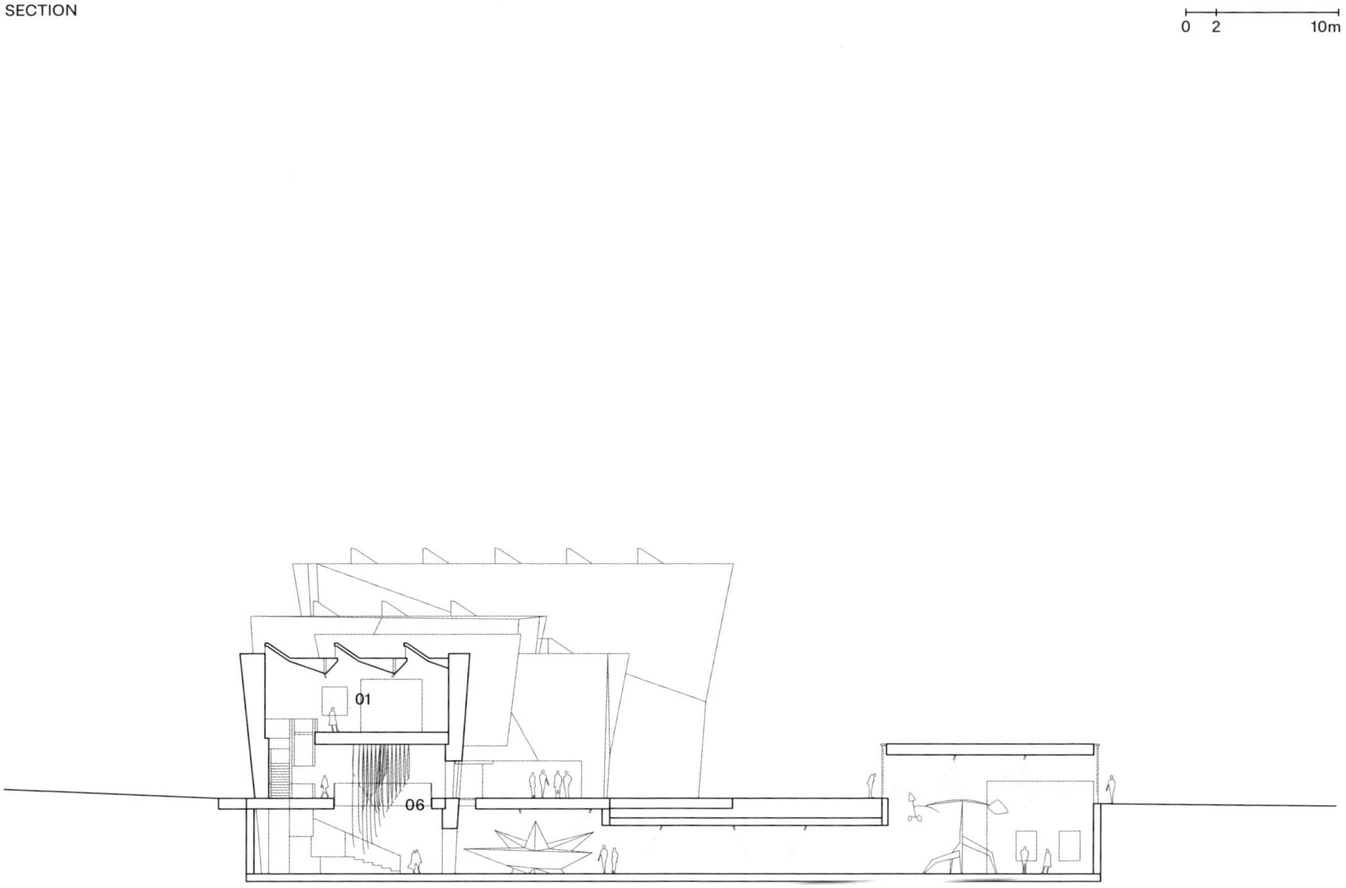


| | | | |
|---|---|---|---|
| 01. | JALAVA GALLERY | 06. | SARA HILDEN ATRIUM |

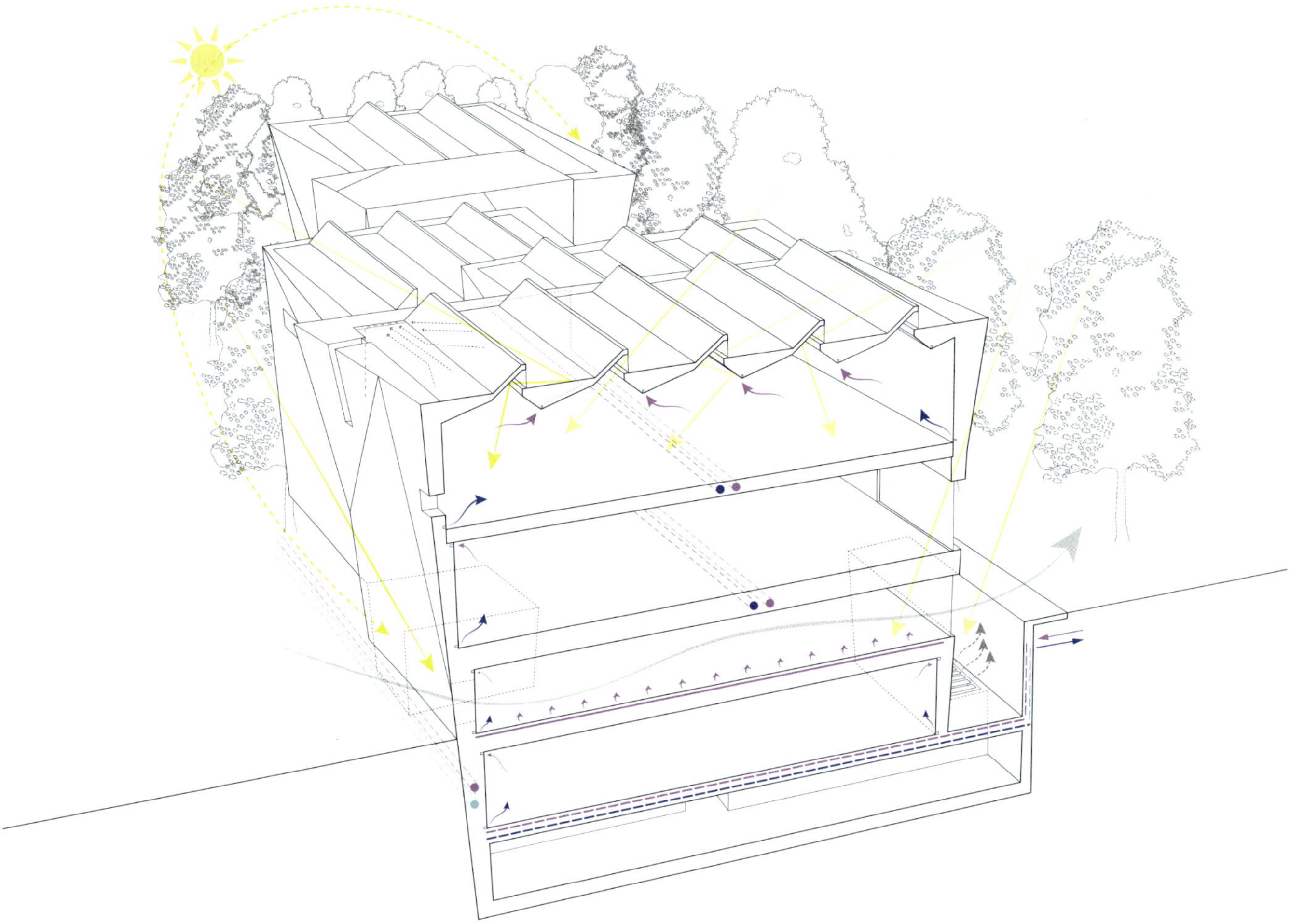

The building creates a permeable treshold between the art and the surrounding nature, breathing in fresh air and filtering natural light in through rooflights.

# TRANSI–
# TIONS

Continuity of space is negotiated by architecture.
Ecotone is a term that refers to a transitional area between two biological communities, the point at which they meet and integrate. An ecotone may appear on the ground as a gradual blending of the two communities across a broad area, or it may manifest itself as a sharp boundary line. Buildings, like these transitional zones, form boundaries between different areas and activities. Thresholds between outside and inside environments, as well as different interior zones, are not only physical but are also shaped by our understanding of private and public spaces. In the framework of Geospaces, we seek, rather than sharp dividing lines, a continuity of space between inside and outside, and a flexibility of functions.

Architectural transitions are defined by culture, climate and technology. The fundamentals of architecture are shelter, warmth, light and comfort. The more extreme climatic conditions are, the more defined the boundaries must be. In milder climates, it becomes easier to maximise fluidity between inside and outside. This applies to both inside-outside relationships and to the meeting point between building and ground. While classical and modernist archetypes separate the building from the ground, creating a hierarchy between human and nature, in contrast, many contexts embody a greater fluidity between nature and architecture. Laugier's "Primitive Hut" theory, which aimed to establish the roots of architecture, projects Classical notions (column and roof structure) onto an imagined natural past. However, diverse forms of habitat and vernacular typologies (treehouses; reed islands; igloos), challenge this narrow definition of the fundamentals of architecture. Geospaces seeks to explore an architecture which subverts the division of building from nature and redefines space, not as a passive condition but as an active agent.

(T)01
Archetypes of relationship between building and ground plinth, raised pilotis

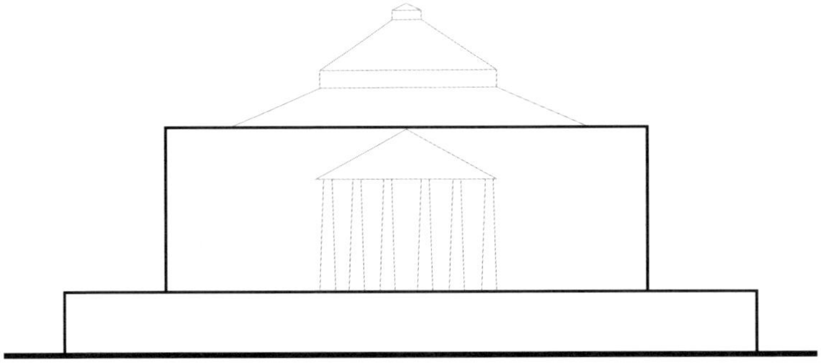

Villa Capra La Rotonda, Palladio

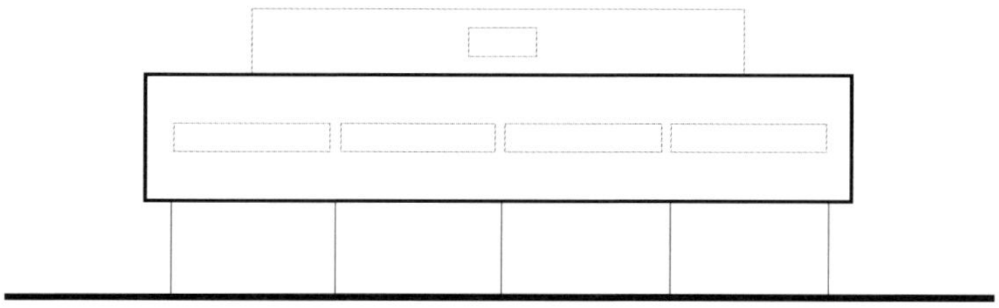

Corbusier, Villa Savoye

# Continuity of negotiated by

(T)02
An Ecotone
Aerial photo of Santo Carlos, Argentina

# space is architecture.

# ECOTONE

(E)01

Ecotone (E) occupies an intermediate space between education and industry, forming part of the Yıldız university campus in İstanbul. The hybrid co-working and education space is part of a campus designed with the intention to spark innovation and the development of new technologies. Rethinking the conditions of Laugier's "Primitive Hut", the design composes an arrangement between column and roof that merge into each other, adapting to its location in a high wind and earthquake risk zone. The structure is self supporting, the slender columns, reminiscent of stalagmites or stalactites, expanding at their ground and roof connections to support side loads.

Ecotone proposes a new examplar for pandemic resistant and sustainable office architecture, with the integration of outside areas and interior planting into the design. Open air fingers in the plan layout provide areas that, weather-dependent, can be used as informal meeting zones, avoiding closed group spaces. As well as these outdoor rooms, planting brings green inside the building, and natural ventilation provides clear air flows throughout the interior spaces, without relying on mechanical systems. The building employs passive geothermal heating and cooling, while water both for drainage and cooling passes through the tubular columns from sky to earth.

(E)02

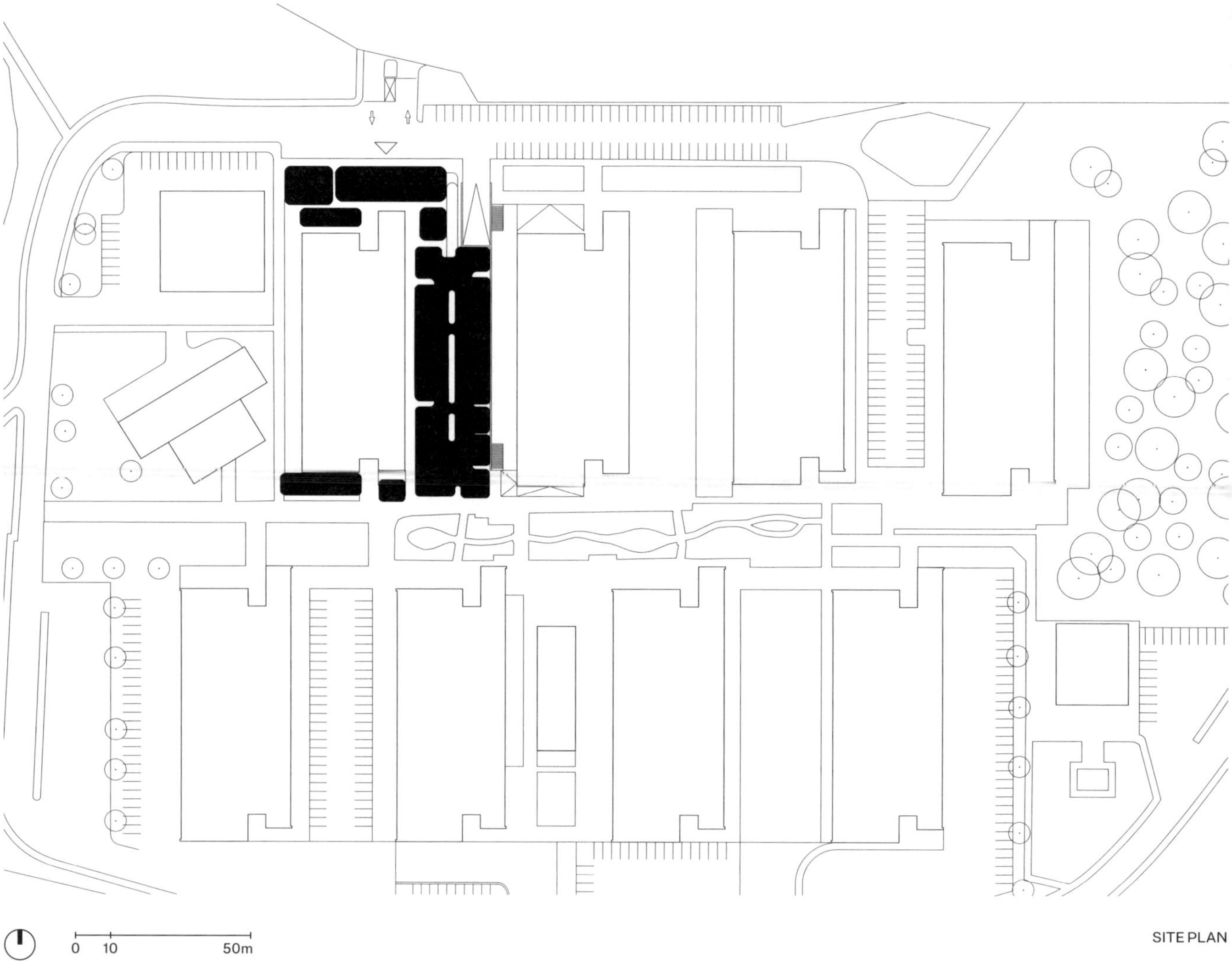


SITE PLAN

Ecotone proposes a new examplar for pandemic resistant and sustainable office architecture, while aiming to achieve a new fundamental relationship between structure and ground.

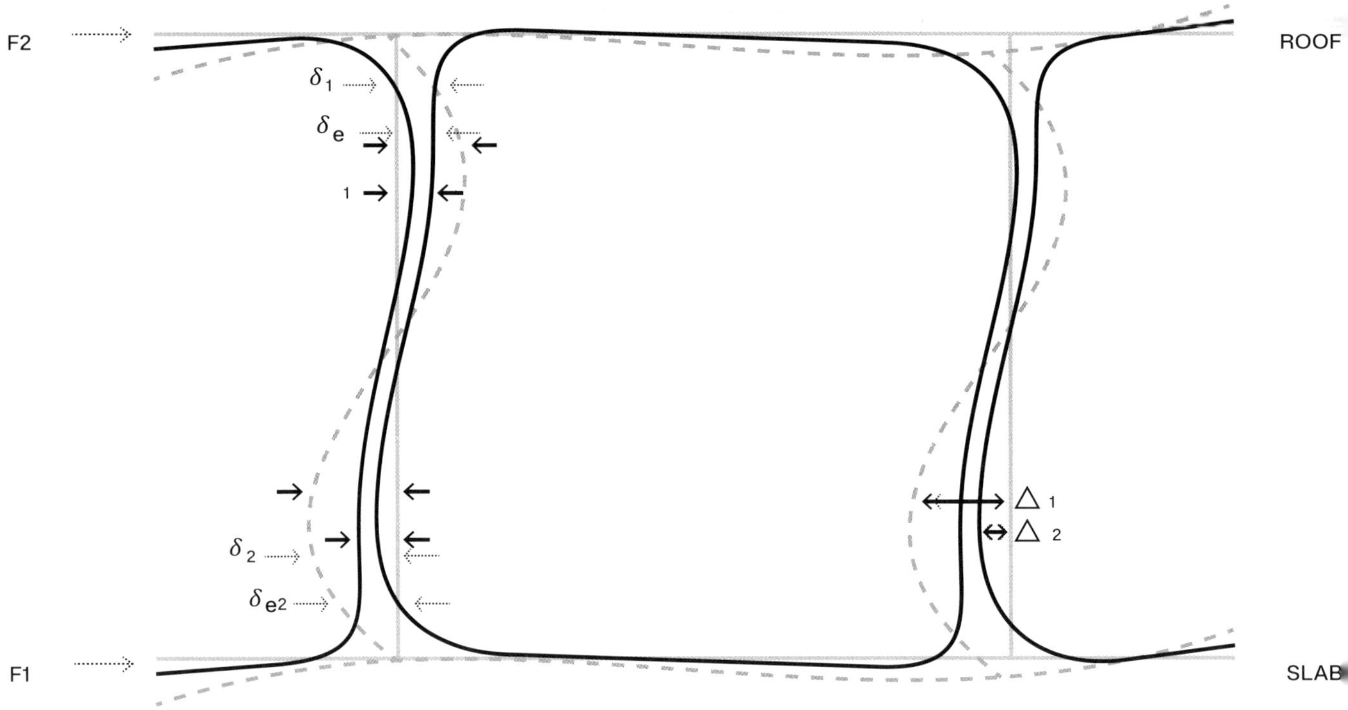
F2
ROOF
$\delta_1$
$\delta_e$
1
$\delta_2$
$\delta_{e2}$
$\triangle$ 1
$\triangle$ 2
F1
SLAB

The building aims to achieve, through a simple structure, a new fundamental relationship between roof and slab.

SECTION

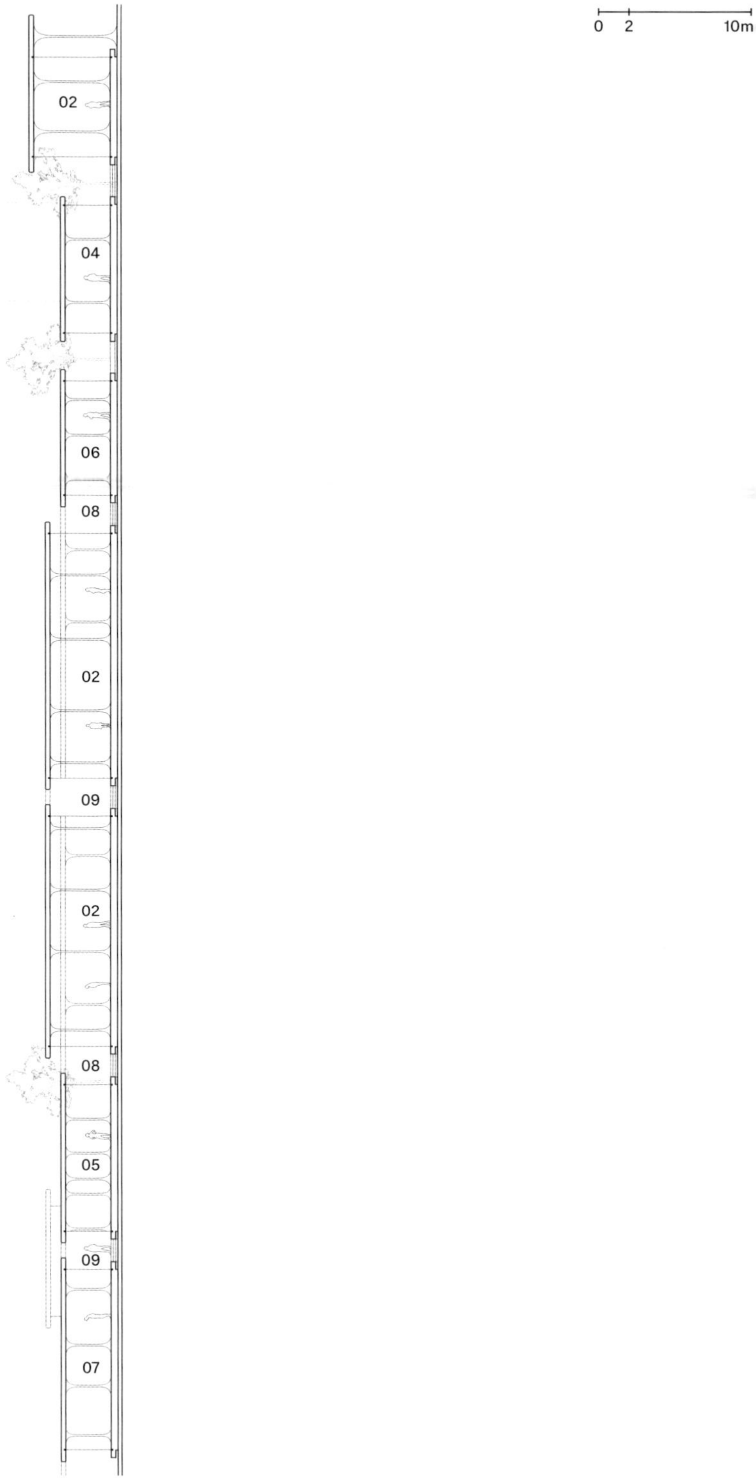


| | | | | | | | |
|---|---|---|---|---|---|---|---|
| 02. | CO-WORKING SPACE | 05. | OPEN OFFICE | 07. | OPEN MEETING ZONE | 09. | OUTSIDE SOCIAL SPACE |
| 04. | CAFE | 06. | LOUNGE AREA | 08. | OUTSIDE MEETING AREA | | |

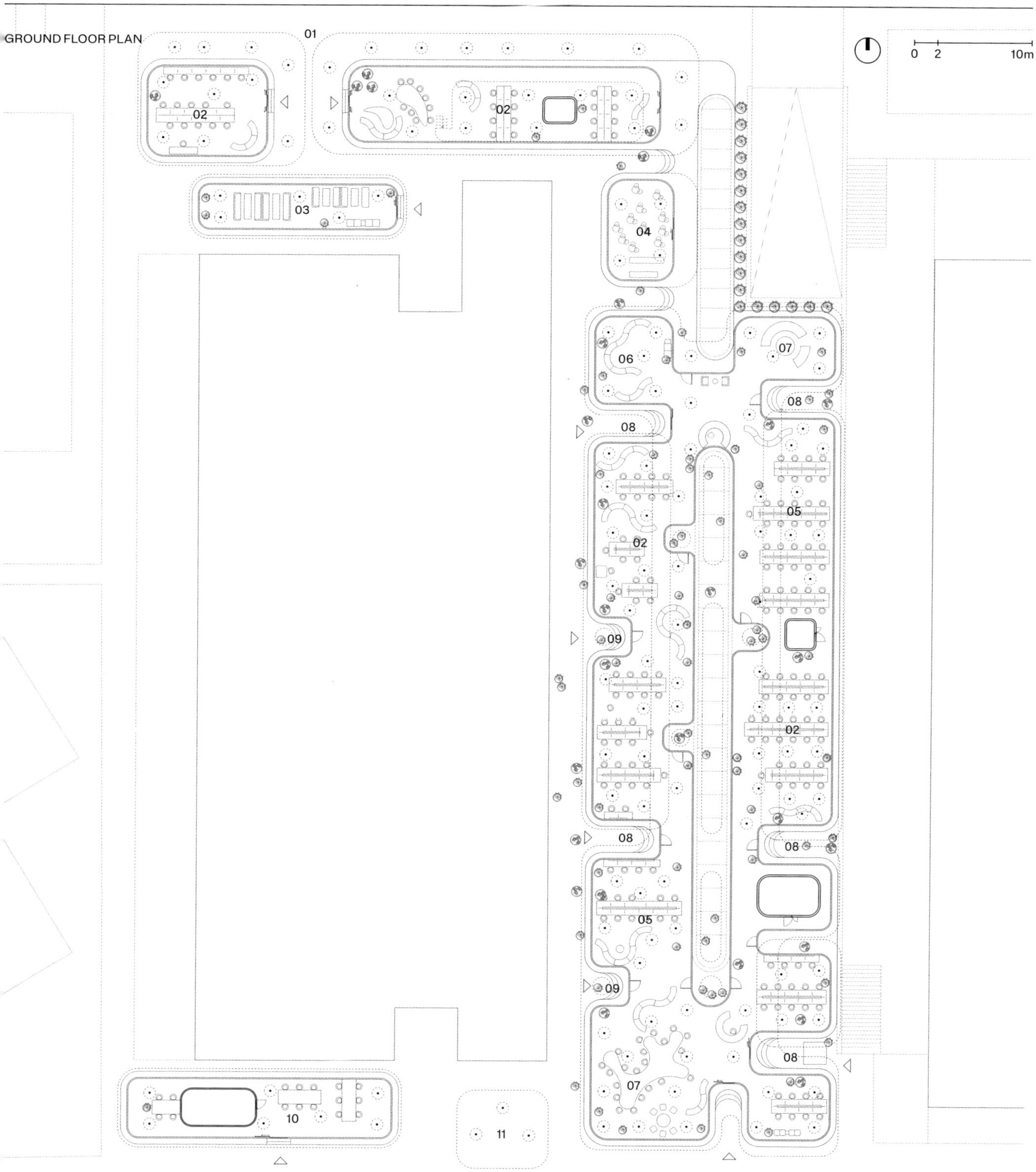


| | | | | | | | |
|---|---|---|---|---|---|---|---|
| 1. | MAIN ENTRANCE | 04. | CAFE | 07. | OPEN MEETING ZONE | 10. | MEETING ROOM |
| 2. | CO-WORKING SPACE | 05. | OPEN OFFICE | 08. | OUTSIDE MEETING AREA | 11. | CANOPY |
| 3. | AI ROOM | 06. | LOUNGE AREA | 09. | OUTSIDE SOCIAL SPACE | | |

# PANORAMA

(P)01

Panorama (P) is a piece of public art that criticizes the lack of public space, and the confused function of the few open, green spaces in the city.

The white hoop hanging "illogically" presents an attractive element that invites the viewer to the platform by proposing a threshold between inside and outside. To be left alone with this white hoop evokes a contradictory state in the backdrop of the beautiful panorama of the coast. Panorama may not be functional or easily grasped, but it presents a happy surprise for everyone who encounters it. The confusion about its functionality enables visitors or accidental guests to establish a complex relationship with the work. Perhaps when the viewer spends enough time, he/she becomes part of the installation, and realizes that he/she is actually participating critically in this attitude that approaches the lustful commodification of views in the city.

The structure had to be built in such a manner as to be easily transportable, as it was going to visit key public spaces in the city. To make it portable, and to give it an "architectural fairground" quality, Panorama was designed to include smaller parts that could be assembled easily. It has been years since Istanbul has lost its harmonic view of ecology that its topography naturally provided. We are hoping that Panorama, by unhealthily replicating the dramatic congestion that the city experienced in the aftermath of the 1980s, emphasises the importance of the inclusion of the remnants of this natural topography into the city.

(P)02

SECTION

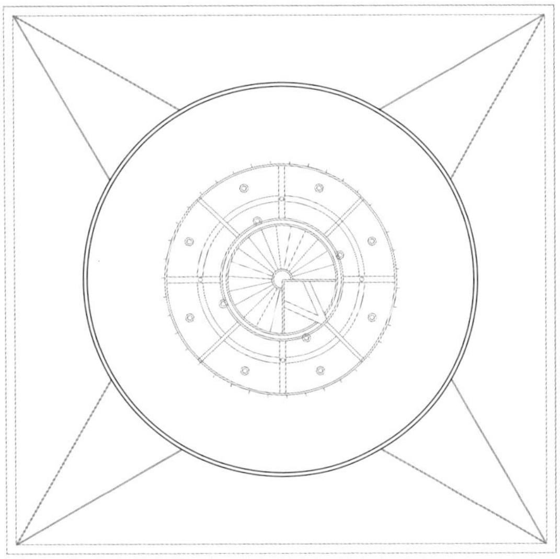

(P)03

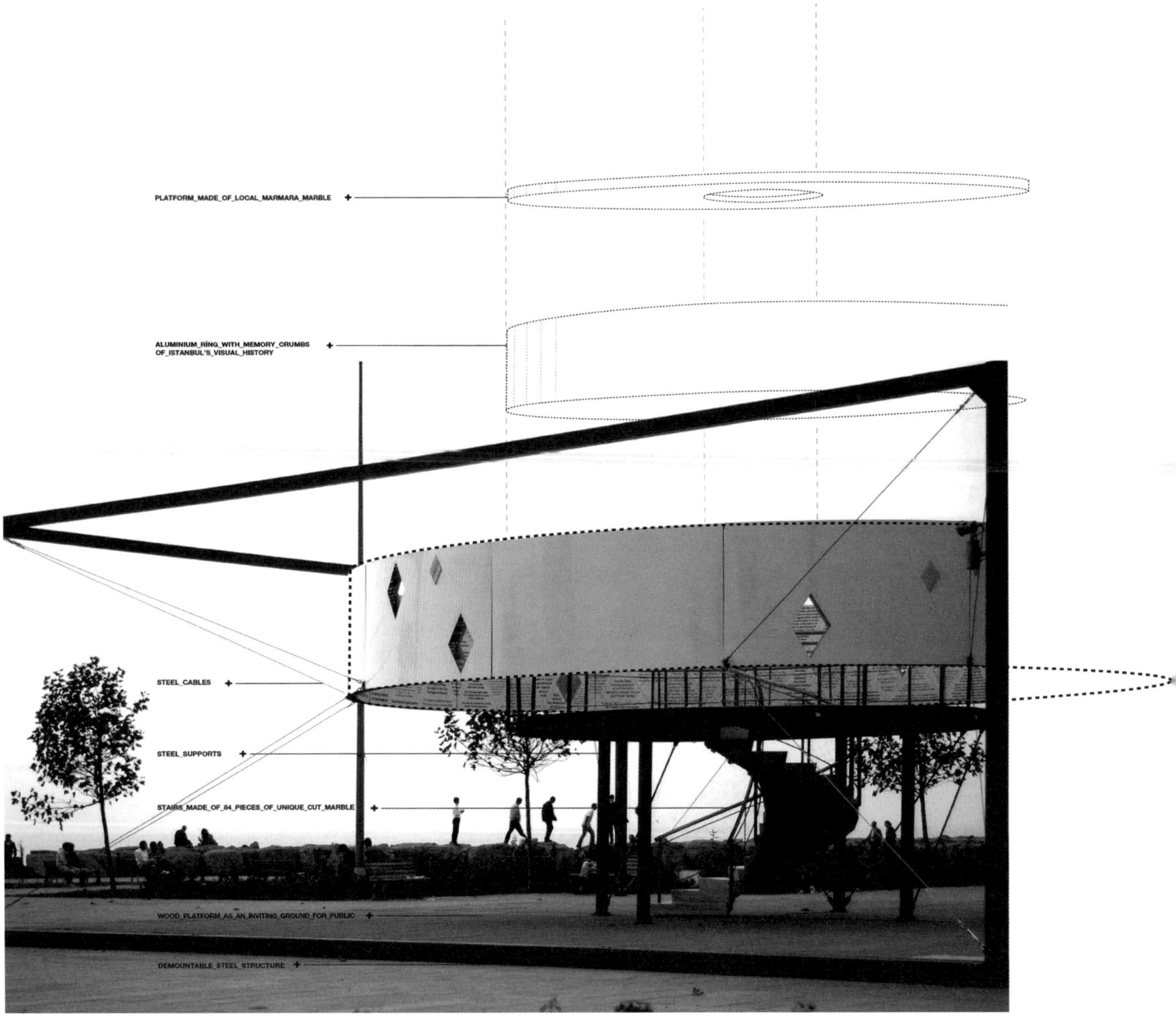
PLATFORM_MADE_OF_LOCAL_MARMARA_MARBLE
ALUMINIUM_RİNG_WITH_MEMORY_CRUMBS
OF_ISTANBUL'S_VISUAL_HISTORY
STEEL_CABLES
STEEL_SUPPORTS
STAIRS_MADE_OF_84_PIECES_OF_UNIQUE_CUT_MARBLE
WOOD_PLATFORM_AS_AN_INVITING_GROUND_FOR_PUBLIC
DEMOUNTABLE_STEEL_STRUCTURE

(P)04

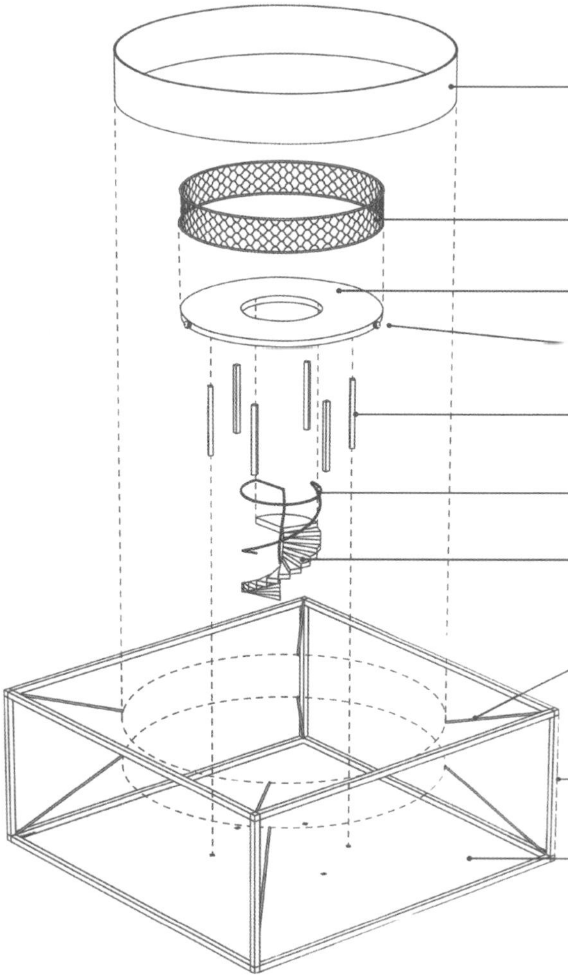
ALUMINUM RING WITH MEMORY CRUMBS OF ISTANBUL'S VISUAL HISTORY
STEEL MESH RAILING
PLATFORM MADE OF LOCAL MARMARA MARBLE
SPOTS TO LID THE HOVERING RING
STEEL SUPPORTS
METAL RAILINGS
STAIRS MADE OF 84 PIECES OF UNIQUE CUT MARBLE
STEEL CABLES FOR HOLDING THE RING
DEMOUNTABLE STEEL STRUCTURE
WOOD PLATFORM AS AN INVITING GROUND FOR PUBLIC

(P)05

# EVOLUTIONS

After all, creatures can only survive with evolution, perhaps it is the same for buildings. When it comes to historical structures, neither complete replacement nor an insistence on maintaining the same dysfunctional archetypes are effective strategies. What if historical structures, rather than simply being preserved or destroyed, were allowed to evolve? In other words, perhaps the best method of preservation is adaptation. We believe an approach based on evolution is a meaningful method of conservation for historic and modern architecture, and even for landscapes. In our work we aim to be part of a process of adaptation which allows architecture to grow and find new purpose.

Cities are like organisms, they can't be scrapped and built from scratch. Urban renewal should be a process of gradual regeneration, like cells replacing themselves in an organ. Historic structures have much longer lifespans than recent constructions, often displaying how they have evolved through different societies in their physical and material qualities. An example that demonstrates this is İstanbul's ancient Theodosian Land Walls, which trace the evolution of the city through their layers of rebuilding, repair and restoration.

An architecture that evolves the historic context can create a better understanding of history while anticipating a relationship to the future. This approach avoids clinging to the nostalgia of precious historic preservation, while maintaining a continuity and connection to history. If we practiced more adaptive reuse we would save many buildings worthy of a longer life, and hugely reduce unnecessary carbon emissions generated by the construction and demolition industries. Evolution as preservation is an approach that can apply not only to buildings, but to the way we shape our streets, neighbourhoods and cities.

(E)01
16th Century map of İstanbul neighborhoods

(E)02
Traces of Byzantine and Ottoman eras in the historic Land Walls

# After all, creatures can o
# perhaps it is the same for

survive with evolution,
ldings.

# FİTAŞ PASSAGE

(FP)01

Fitaş Passage (FP) is an adaptive reuse project that reclaims a historic arcade space while seeking a new relationship to the street.

The project brings new life to the existing mid-60s building, architecturally unremarkable yet holding a significant place in collective memory due to the cultural activities it has accommodated over the years. Fitaş Passage is located on İstiklal Street, a vibrant pedestrian axis in the heart of İstanbul that has witnessed many changes over the years. Its once-distinctive street facades with vertical sign boards and passages have become flattened by the ubiquity of the generic shop window, whilst the diversity of activities and cultural functions in the street has also declined.

The intervention seeks to pay homage to the distinctive spatial qualities of İstiklal and revitalise the building's relationship to the street, delivering a new facade and new cultural and entertainment facilities including a 2000-seat concert hall, cinema halls, recording studios, a sports centre and dining areas. The interrelationship of the different functions between floors is crucial, reflected in the facade openings, which are positioned according to the activities inside. The interior street of the passage typology is renewed, while the facade is shaped as an articulated interface with intermediate spaces and balconies creating connections to İstiklal Street at every level.

Taksim Square
Tarlabaşı Boulevard
Ana Cesmesi Street
Kurabiye Street
Zambak Street
Bekar Street
Mis Street
İmam Adnan Street
İstiklal Street
Meşelik Street
Sıraselviler Street
0 10 50m

SITE PLAN

The intervention seeks to pay homage to the distinctive spatial qualities of İstiklal and revitalise the building's relationship to the street.

(FP)02
Urban Grain of passageways
on İstiklal Street

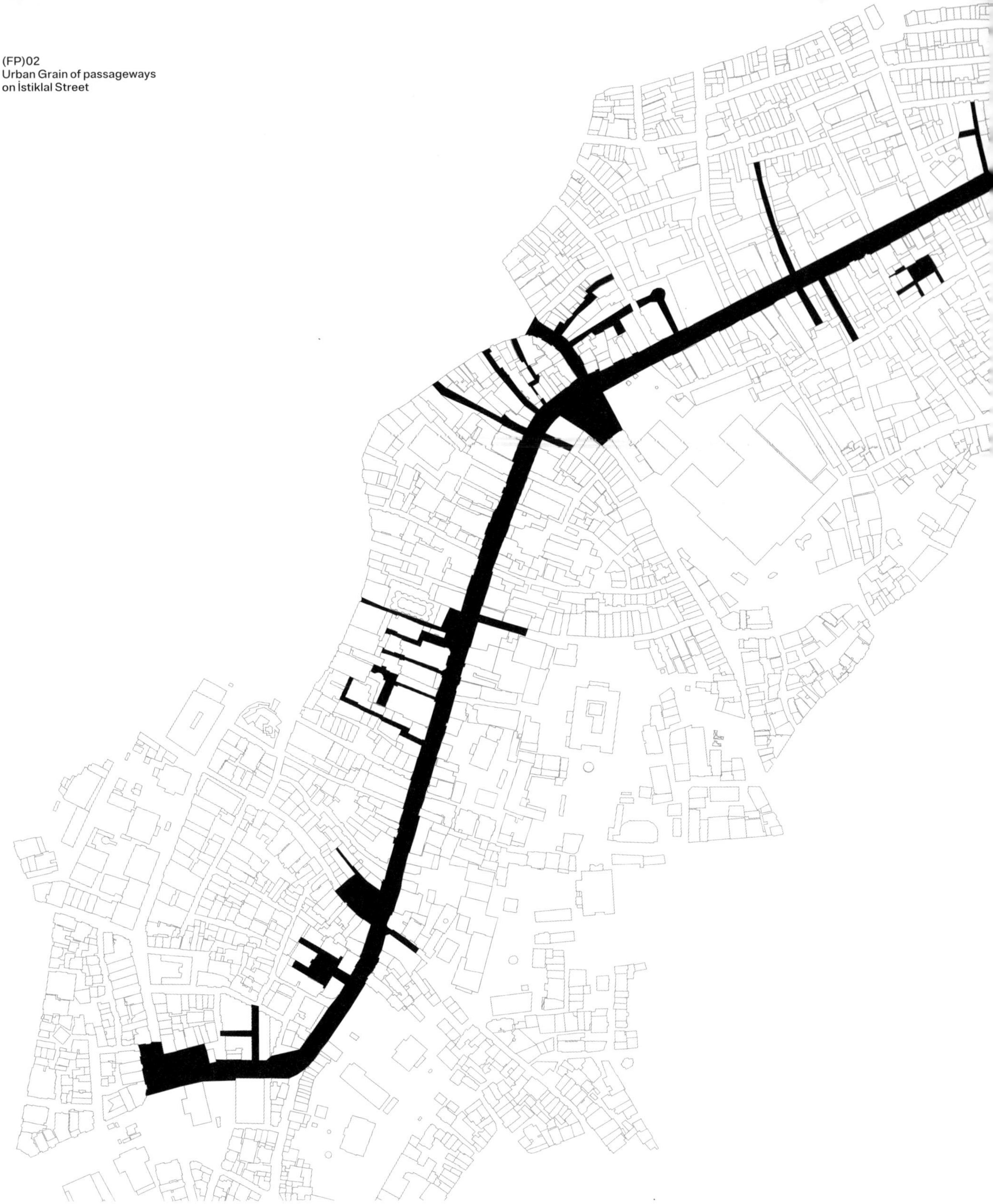

(FP)03
İstiklal Street's vertical signboards
in the 1970s

(FP)04

GROUND FLOOR PLAN

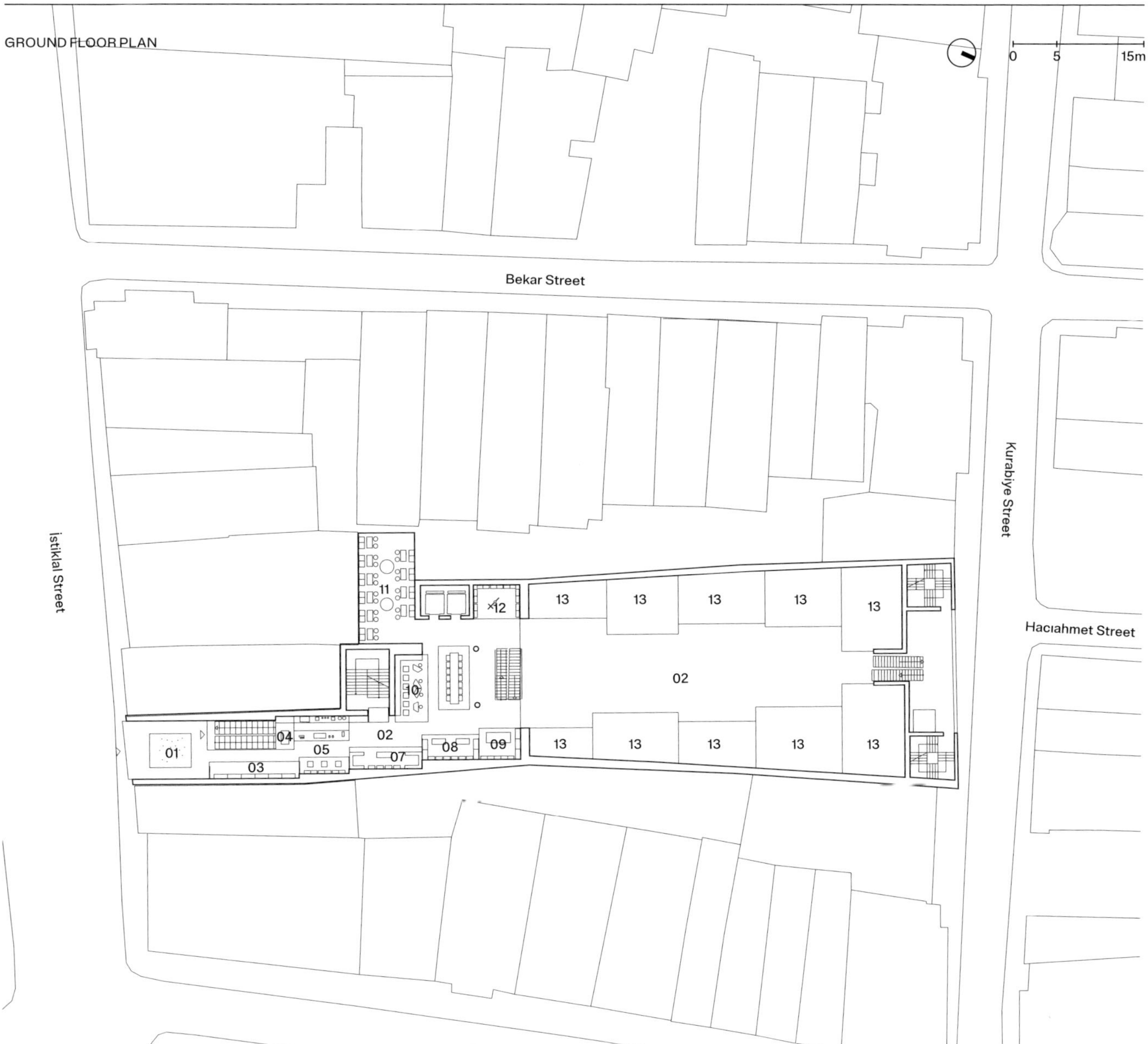


| | | | | | | | |
|---|---|---|---|---|---|---|---|
| 01. | ENTRANCE | 05. | COFFEE SHOP | 09. | FLOWER SHOP | 13. | STORES |
| 02. | STREET PASSAGE | 06. | MAGAZINES | 10. | COMMON TABLE | | |
| 03. | INTERACTION AREA | 07. | BOOK STORE | 11. | COURTYARD | | |
| 04. | COOKIES | 08. | BOUTIQUE | 12. | BIKE SHOP | | |

SECTION PLAN

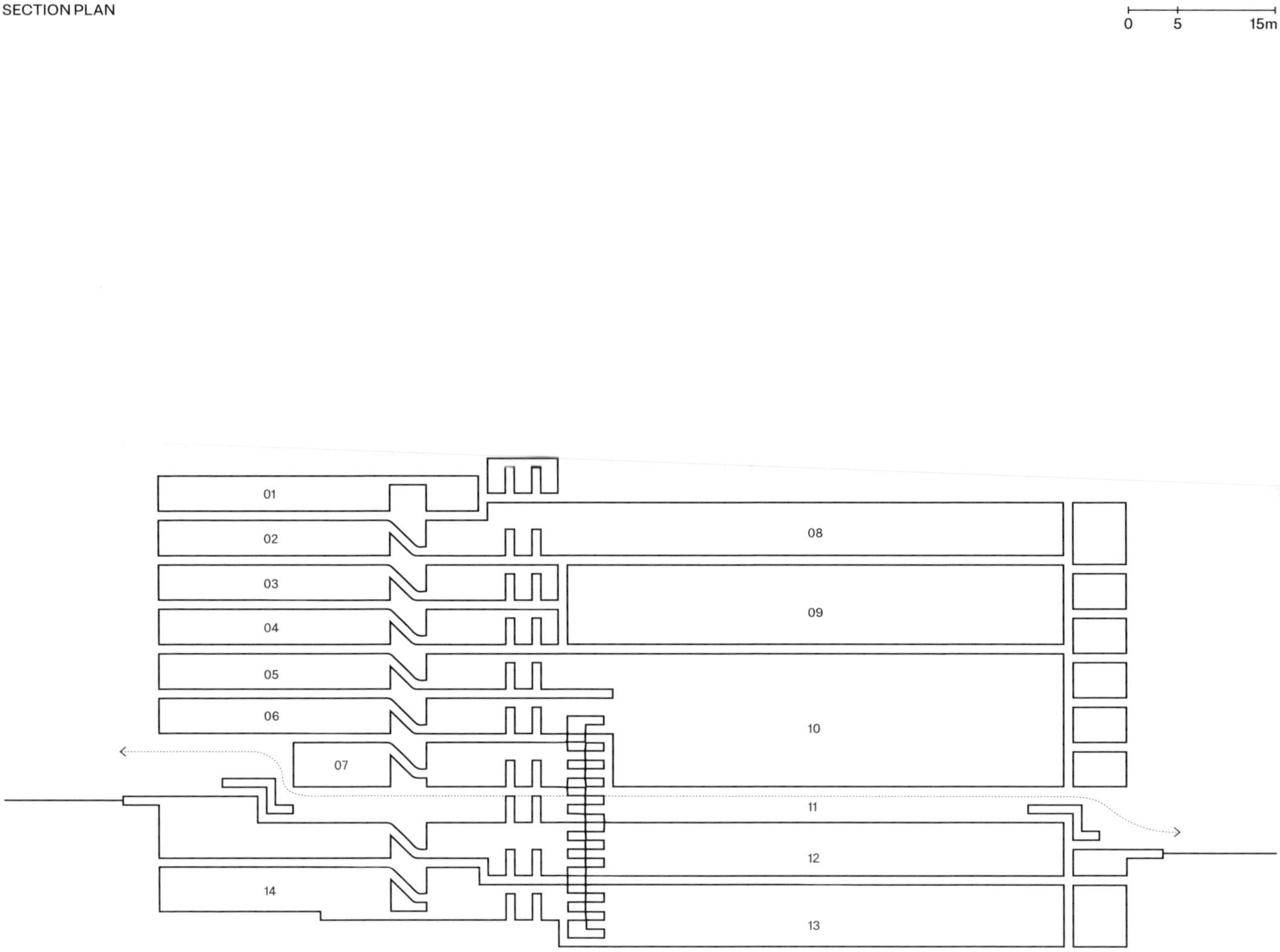


| | | | | | | | |
|---|---|---|---|---|---|---|---|
| 01. | ENTRANCE | 05. | COFFEE SHOP | 09. | FLOWER SHOP | 13. | STORES |
| 02. | STREET PASSAGE | 06. | MAGAZINES | 10. | COMMON TABLE | | |
| 03. | INTERACTION AREA | 07. | BOOK STORE | 11. | COURTYARD | | |
| 04. | COOKIES | 08. | BOUTIQUE | 12. | BIKE SHOP | | |

FACADE DETAIL SKETCH, SUNLIGHT
THROUGH STREET BALCONY

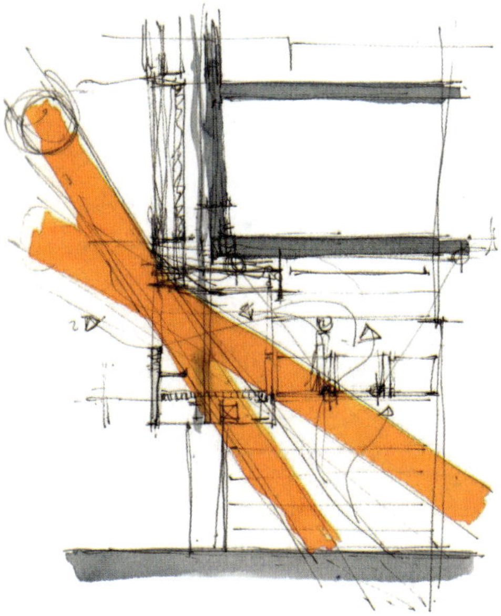

(FP)05

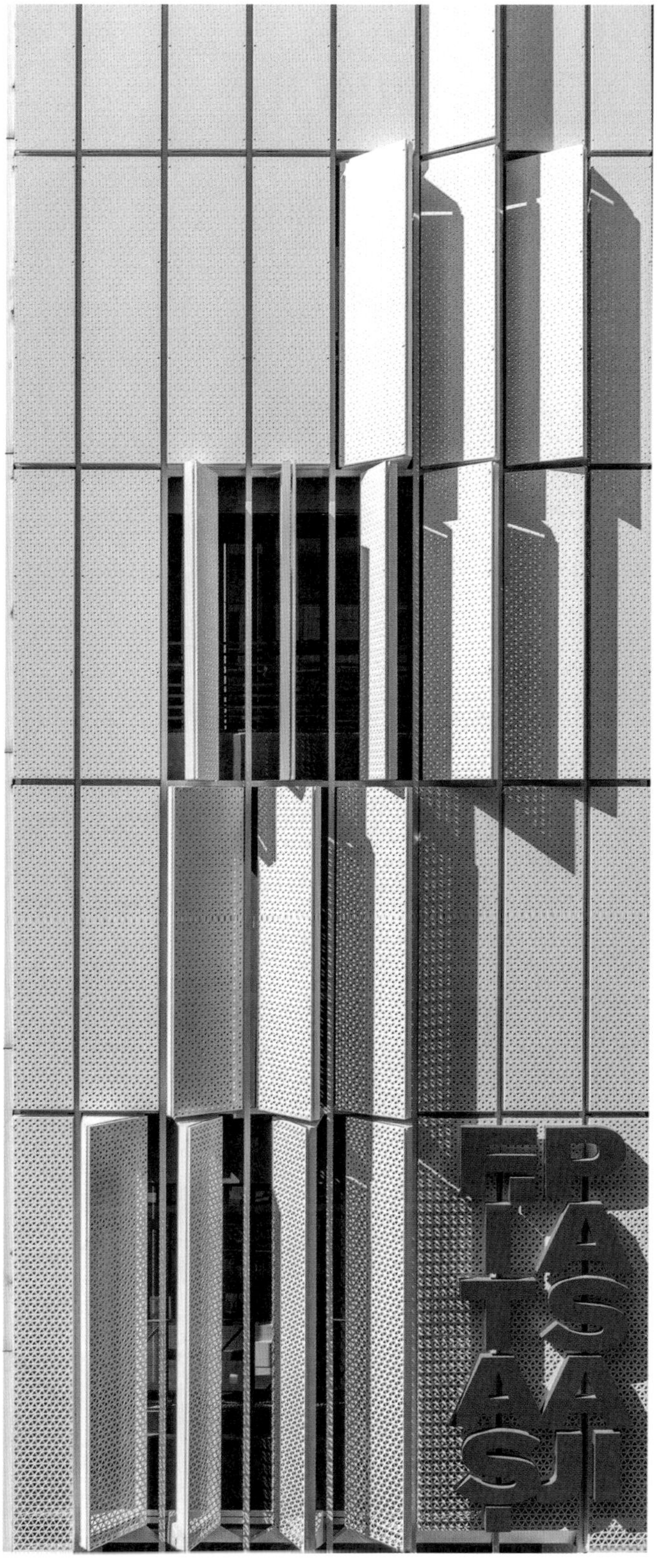

(FP)06

# MUSEUM OF İSTANBUL

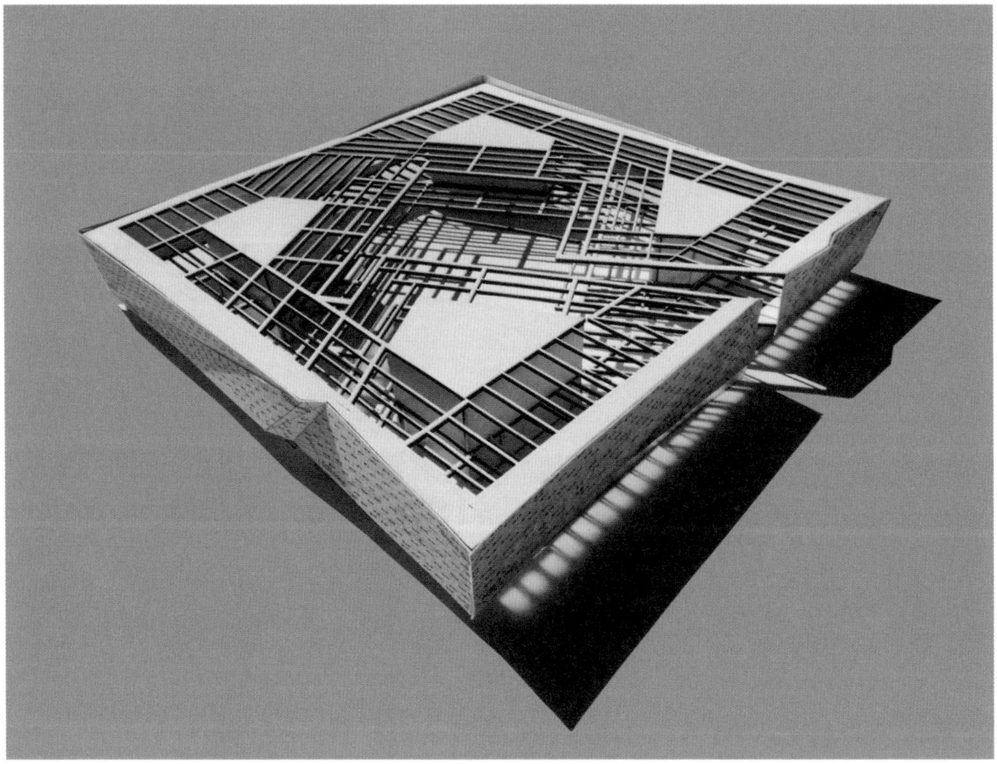

(MI)01
The museum structure is closely integrated with the spatial arrangement, curating a continuous exhibition route

The Museum of İstanbul (Mİ) links the historic city's land walls to a modern transportation hub in the Topkapı area, aiming to activate a public space that connects the history of the city with contemporary society, and to renew the neglected neighbourhood that surrounds the ancient walls.

The building is located in the UNESCO Theodosian Land Walls zone near the threshold of the ancient and the modern city. In this archaeologically sensitive site, the building is constructed inside the existing excavation area of the former bus station. The museum links the historic topography to the contemporary urban dynamics, forming a new axis from the land walls to the modern infrastructure hub. Located within a park, the museum is transparent from all sides in the ground floor, with an entrance bridge guiding visitors into the internal courtyard at first floor level. The visitor enters through a giant crack, like they are walking through an archaeological ruin. The multifaceted facade seeks for a dialogue with the multilayered Theodosian Land Walls. Developed through computational design, using a custom algorithmic script, the facade is composed of a unique, mass customized panellisation pattern that creates the sense of a fragmented monolith. The exterior skin employs an open joint paneling system with a bespoke finish designed to amplify the sky and colour the building in different hues.

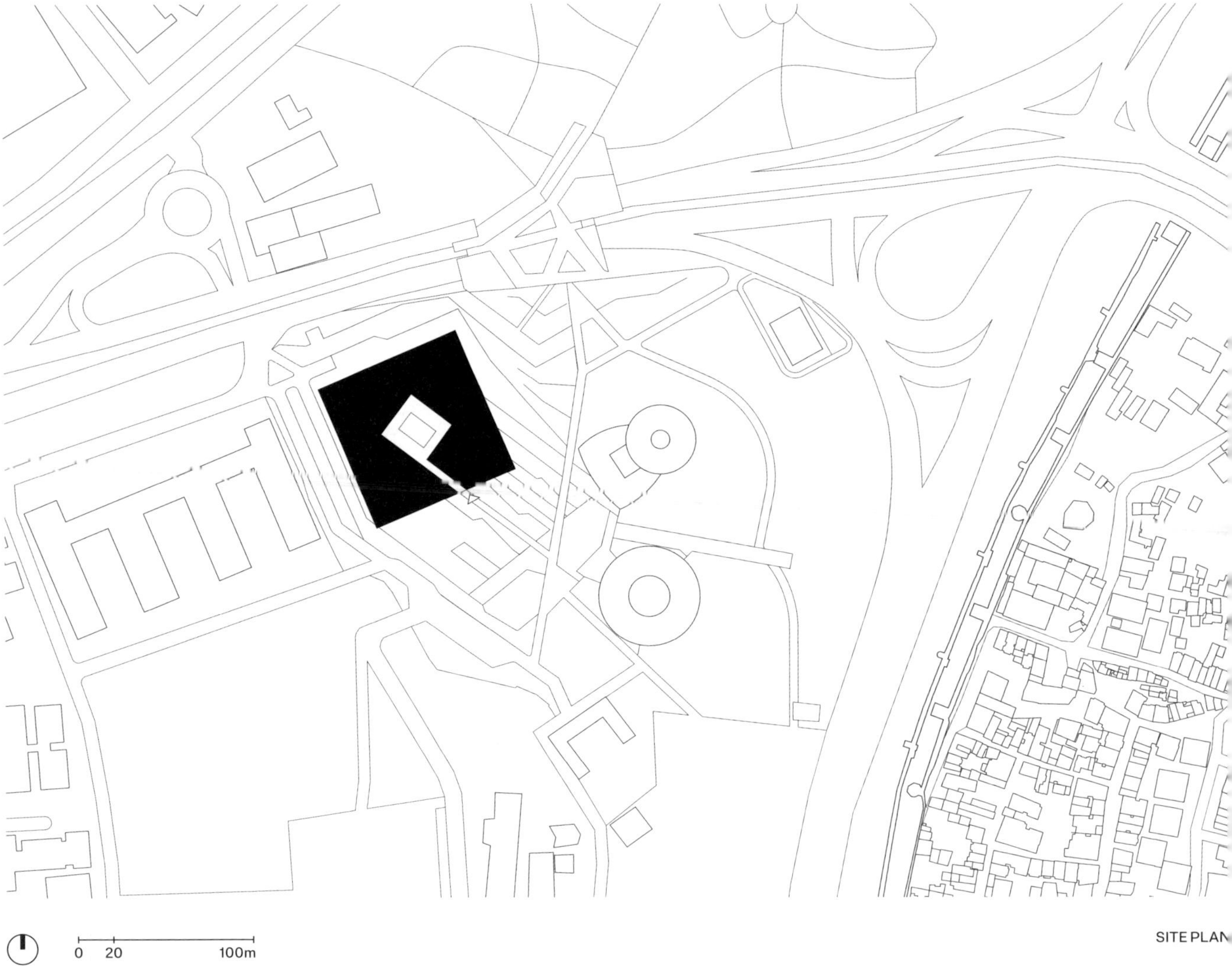


SITE PLAN

The elevated monolith links the historic topography to the contemporary urban dynamics by drawing a line from the ancient land walls to the modern infrastructure hub.

SECTION

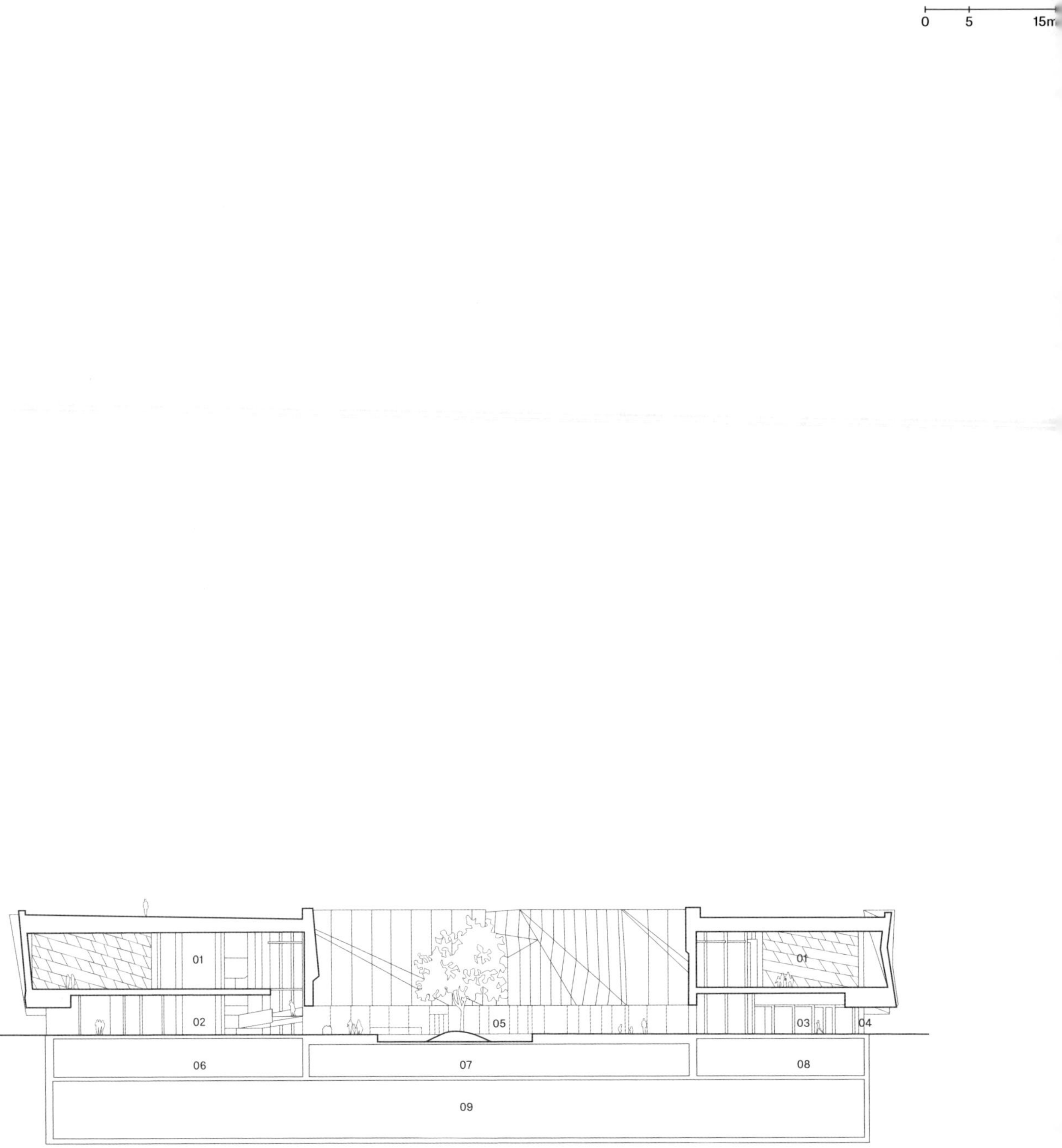


| | | | | | |
|---|---|---|---|---|---|
| 01. | PERMANENT EXHIBITION | 04. | FOYER | 07. | LABORATORIES |
| 02. | CHILDRENS WORKSHOP | 05. | COURTYARD | 08. | SERVICES |
| 03. | LIBRARY | 06. | ARCHIVE | 09. | PUBLIC PARKING |

(MI)03
Model photograph

(MI)04
Site photo, building the panellised facade

(MI)05
Facade technology,
parametrically-designed bespoke panels
minimise contruction waste

Angle A - L (parenthesis is the current angle) on Unfolded Form

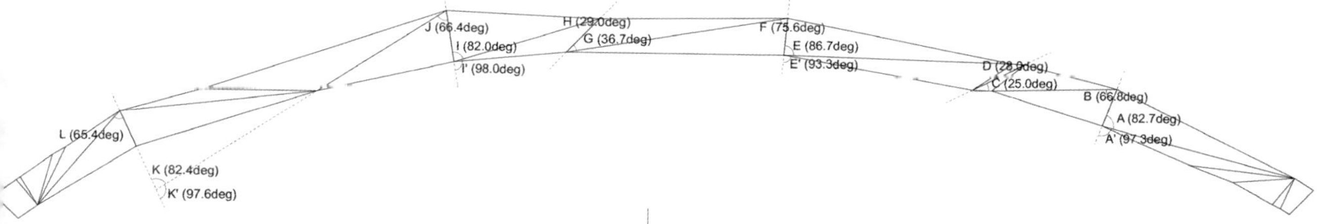


Angle A - L (parenthesis is the current angle)

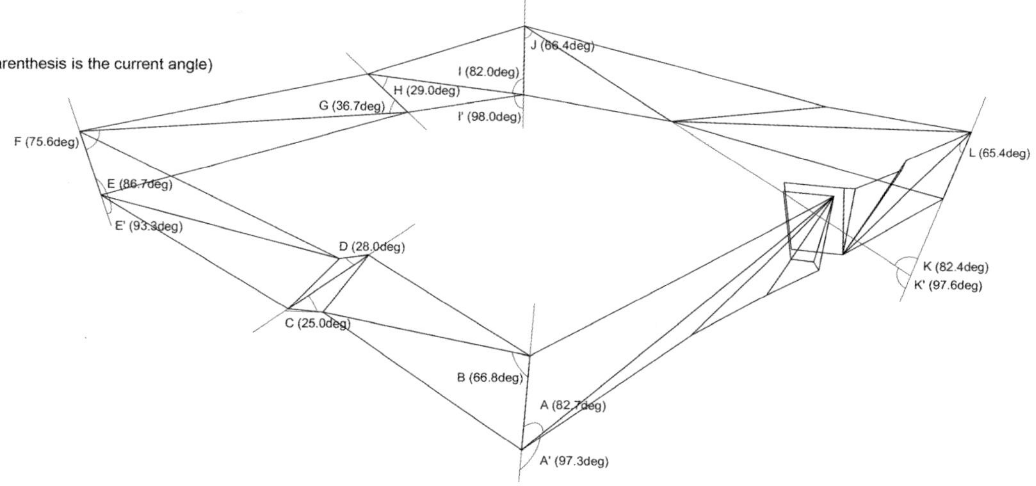

(MI)06
Construction site entrance bridge leads into the courtyard

GROUND FLOOR PLAN

| | | | | | | | |
|---|---|---|---|---|---|---|---|
| 01. | ENTRANCE | 04. | GEOGRAPHIES OF İSTANBUL | 06. | LIFE OF PLACES | 09. | A GLOBAL MEGAPOLIS |
| 02. | READING ROOM | 05. | HISTORY AND SYMBOLS OF THE CITY | 07. | CONSTRUCTIONS | | |
| 03. | FROM THE SEA TO THE CITY | | | 08. | BIRTH OF MODERN CITY | | |

# FUTURE

"Art comes from the future."
Timothy Morton

We see architecture not as an artificial entity but as a new nature. After all, we humans are simply creatures building and adapting our habitats. Feral ecosystems respond and evolve according to their surroundings, whether they are forests or cities. The question we pose is how, through architecture, we can shape the future-nature that we want to move towards. We believe the desirable future is one where making, technology and ecology coincide; an existence in continuity with history, with nature and with earth.

Technology is constantly transforming processes within design, construction, learning, and countless other areas. Interaction between different practices is increasingly possible as a result of this streamlining. We explore interdisciplinary projects that question the point where art and science collide, and the point they might reach in the future. These projects anticipate an entangled future where architecture and cities are shaped by technology and interactions between complex systems. In our Learning Sky project, for example, we propose that learning through making will be the future of knowledge, and hybrid fabrication the future of construction.

Understanding the city as a habitat, we propose that flexible, hybrid technologies of making can shape a common urban and architectural language that constitutes a new nature.

# HYBRIDS

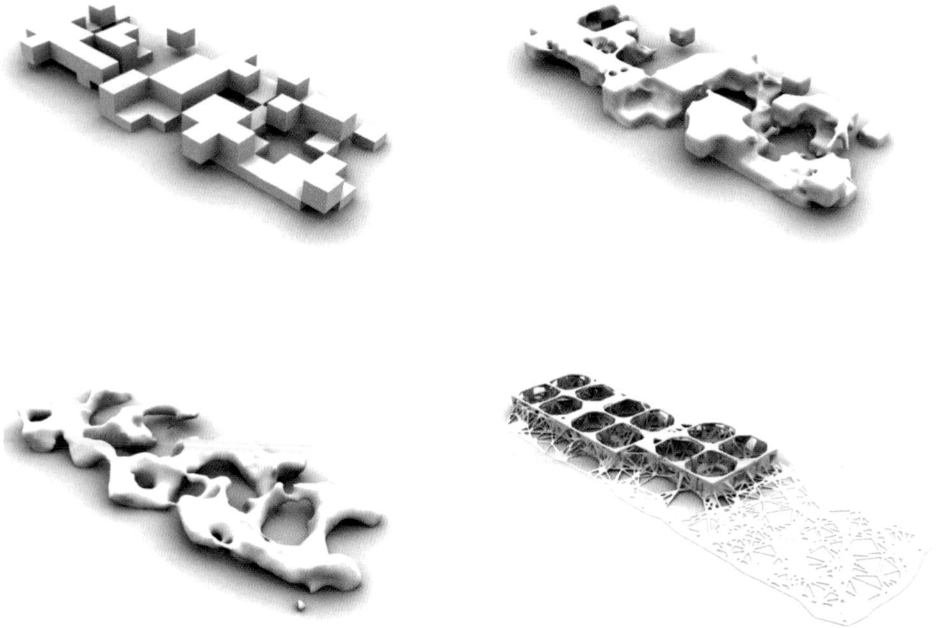

(FH)01
Generative design iterations for Ecotone

(FH)02
Museum of Unlimited Growth,
Le Corbusier

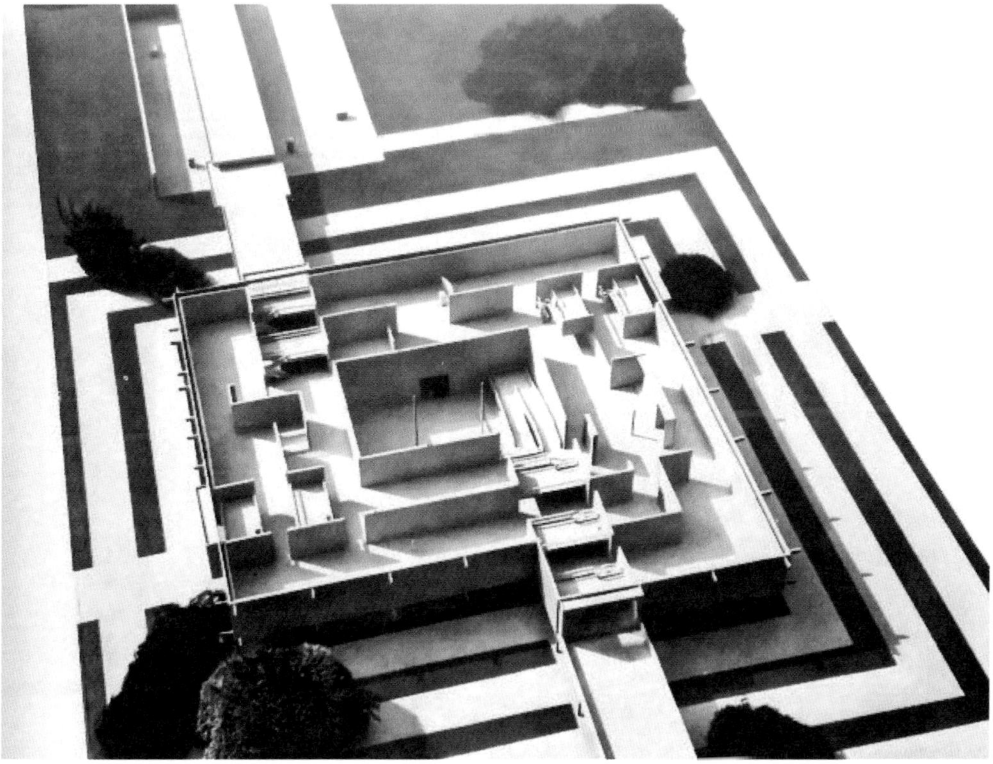

Understanding the city a
flexible, hybrid technolog
a common urban and arc
constitutes a new nature

habitat, we propose that
of making can shape
ctural language that

# AUGMENTED STRUCTURES

(AS)01
Model of parametric facade structure

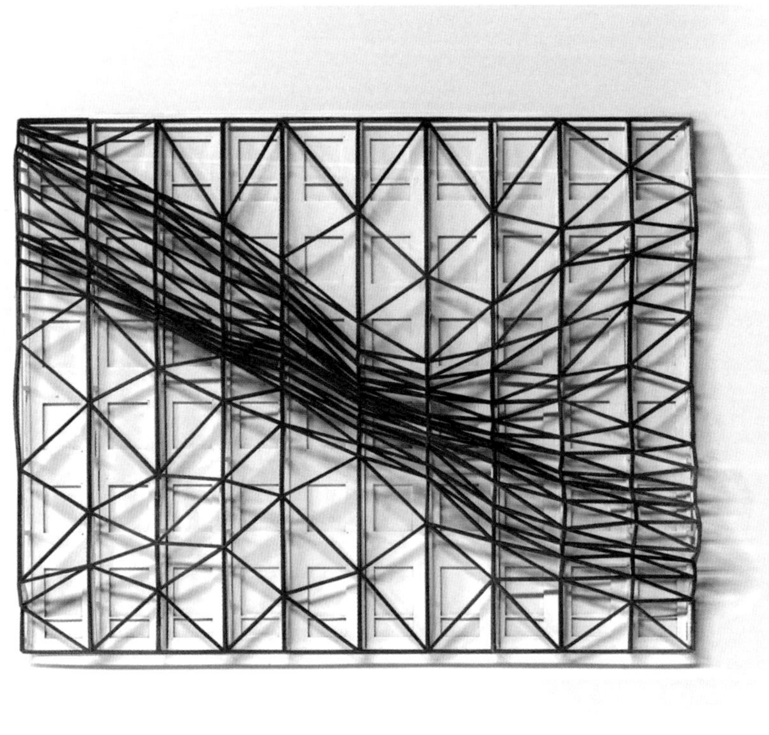

The first phase of the Augmented Structures (AS) project with the Augmented Structures v1.1. Acoustic Formations / İstiklal Street exhibition, reanimates phenomena (sound, architecture and visual arts) that may appear completed and concluded, but in fact are in a continuous process of development, change and transformation.

The project combines disparate disciplines like sound, architecture and the visual arts, allowing them to interact with one another to such a degree that it is impossible to separate them. While the project reexamines the world in visual and aesthetic terms in its capacity as an interdisciplinary transformation project, it also questions the point where art and architecture stand today, and the point they might reach in the future.

This is a project that creates a living canvas while confronting the viewer with a new multilayered media experience, produces sounds, moves and breathes. The performance took place on the Galatasaray façade of Yapı Kredi Cultural Centre, one of the urban landmarks on İstiklal Street, one of İstanbul's most lively and popular arteries. Blending the city's own layers with those of differing disciplines, the performance celebrates their transformation into a multi-layer new media artwork as urban experience.

(AS)03
Field recordings of İstiklal Street are transformed into architectural form

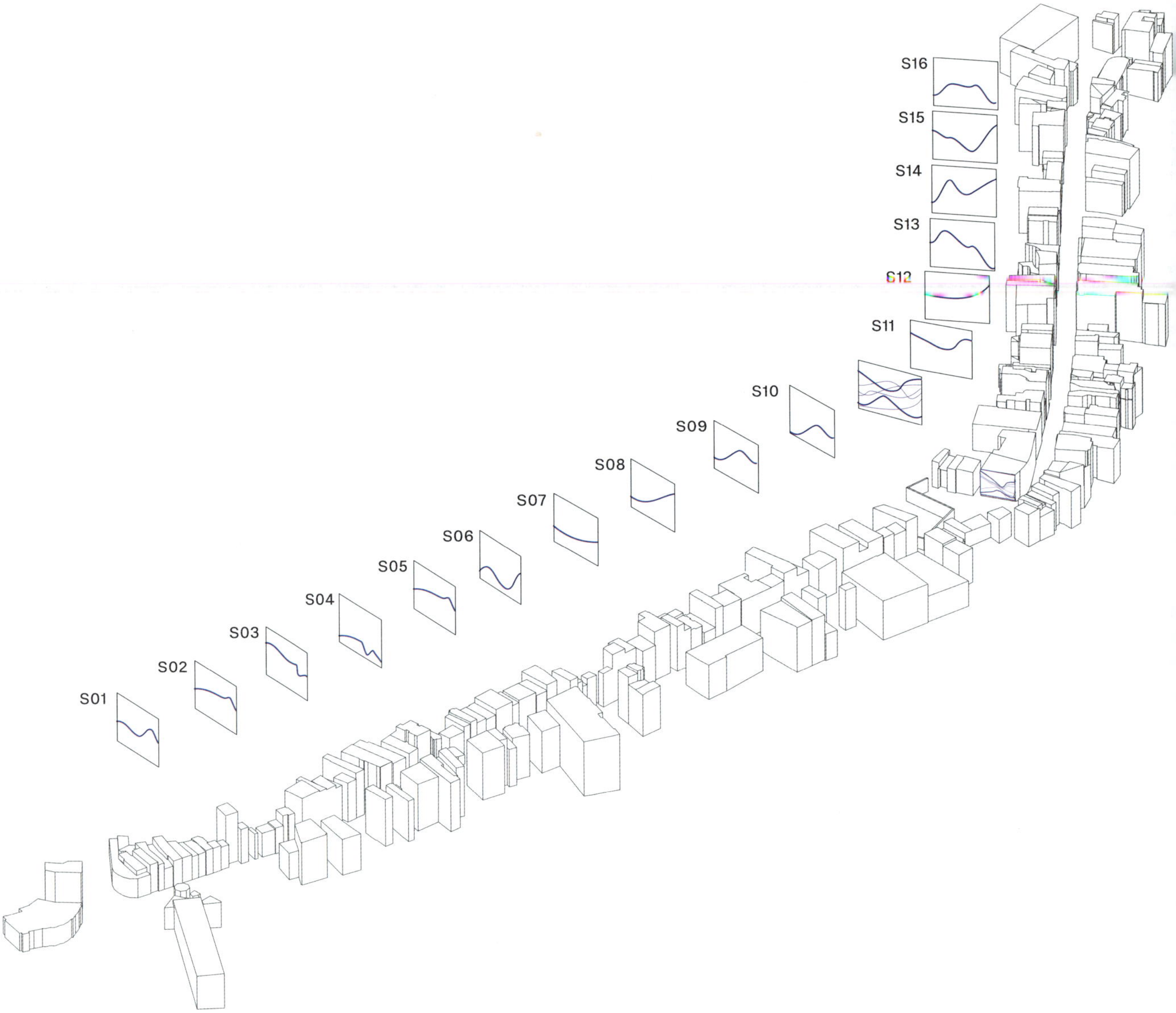

(AS)04
The facade is brought to life by projected animations

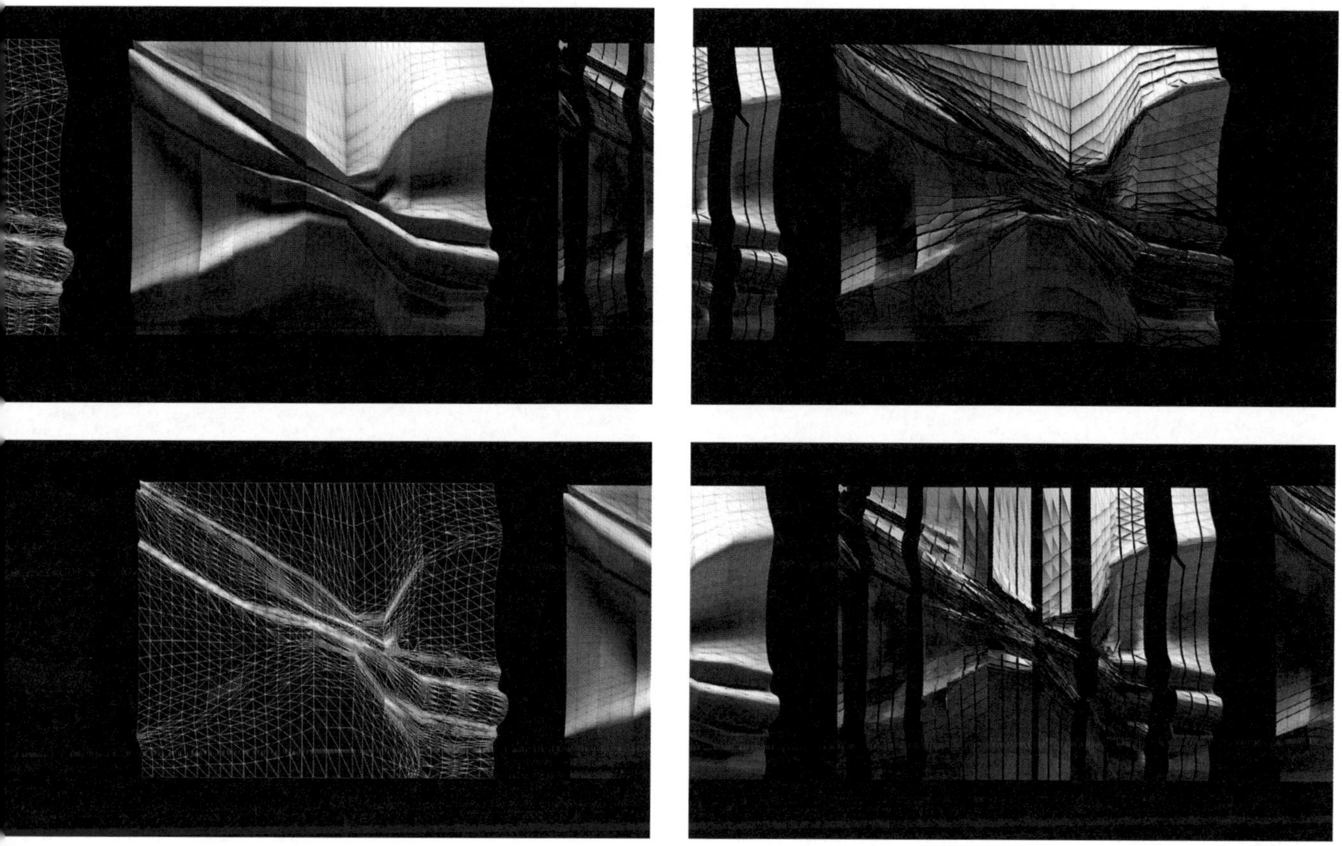

The project invites each discipline to alter its own material state transforming sound into mathematics, mathematics into architecture and architecture into a living canvas.

DIGITAL FABRICATION
METHOD

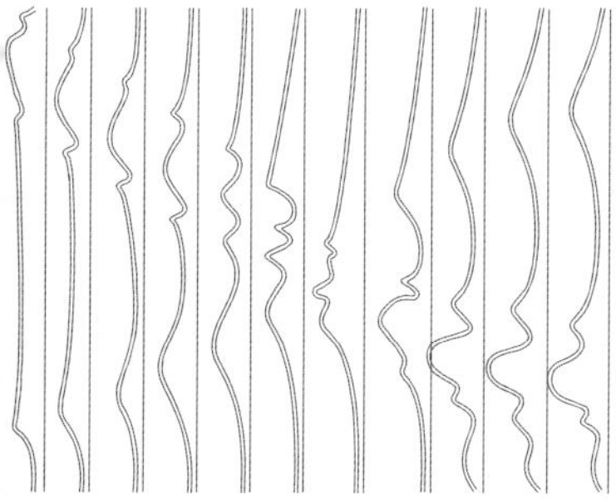

1

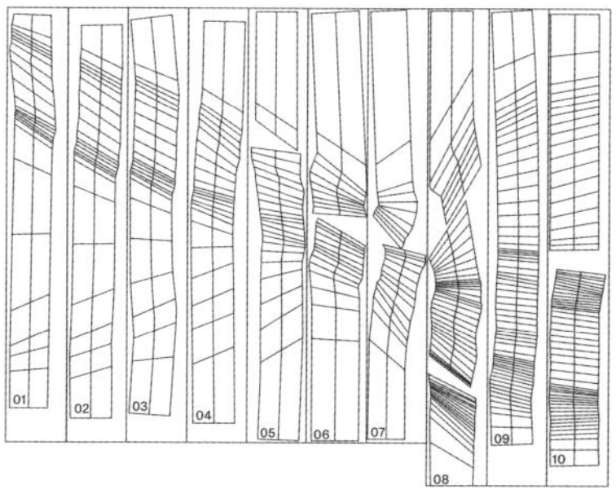


2

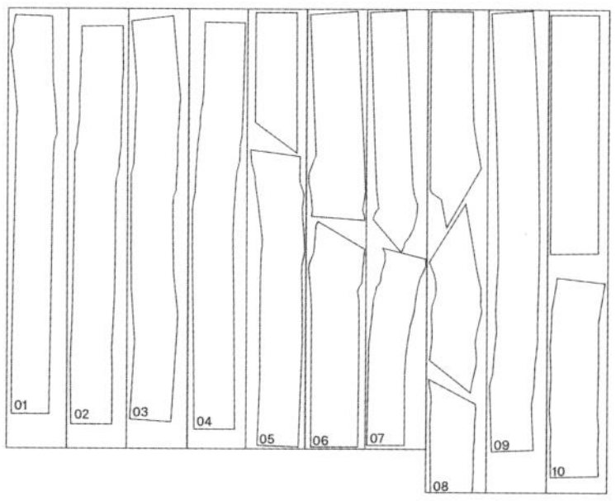


3

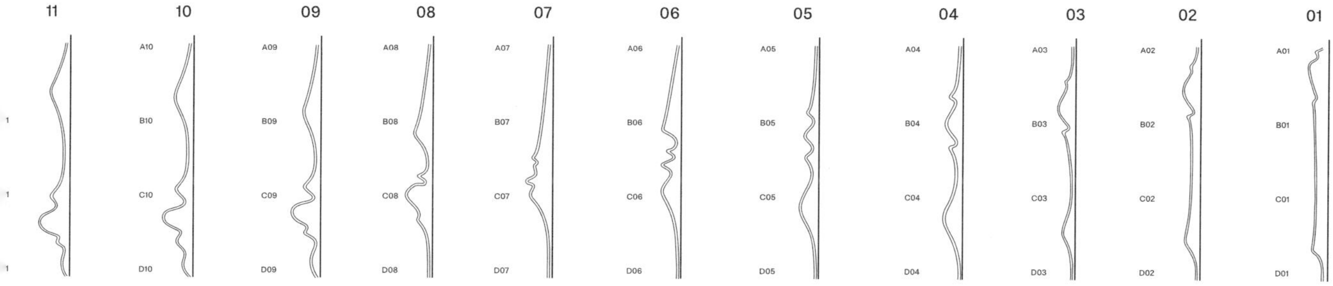


1. SPINES
2. CONNECTION PLANS
3. UNROLLED SURFACES

# LEARNING SKY

(LS)01
Learning sky, the library is punctured by openings to the outside

Learning Sky (LS) proposes a habitat for education and innovation at the heart of Songdo city; a habitat for future learners and a flexible space in which knowledge, making and technology intermingle. The evolution of Songdo is anticipated as a city of education in which the library is not just a space for passive learning, but an environment that will facilitate the construction of new knowledge and ideas.

The library emerges as an extension and continuation of the ground, tracing the ecological heritage of the local tidal flats and proposing an alternative urban texture that is closely integrated with nature, in contrast to the surrounding cityscape with its high rise urban blocks and large setbacks. The low building is like an earthscape that draws visitors in from each side and creates a series of internal gardens. The hybrid structure is composed of 3D-printed concrete cores creating enclosed spaces that support a lightweight timber roof.

The construction of the library is informed by a philosophy of learning by making. The innovative fabrication method emphasizes the relationship between reading, learning, creating and constructing. 3D printing technology and form-making defines the central fractal-like concrete structures that emerge from the ground and define enclosed spaces within. Echoing the transformative effects of the Renaissance printing press on the accessibility and transmission of knowledge, the 3D printing process has the potential to transform construction and many aspects of life by translating information – code or pattern – into physical form. The future is a future of making, where knowledge, craftsmanship and creativity are united in hybrid forms of knowledge.

(LS)02

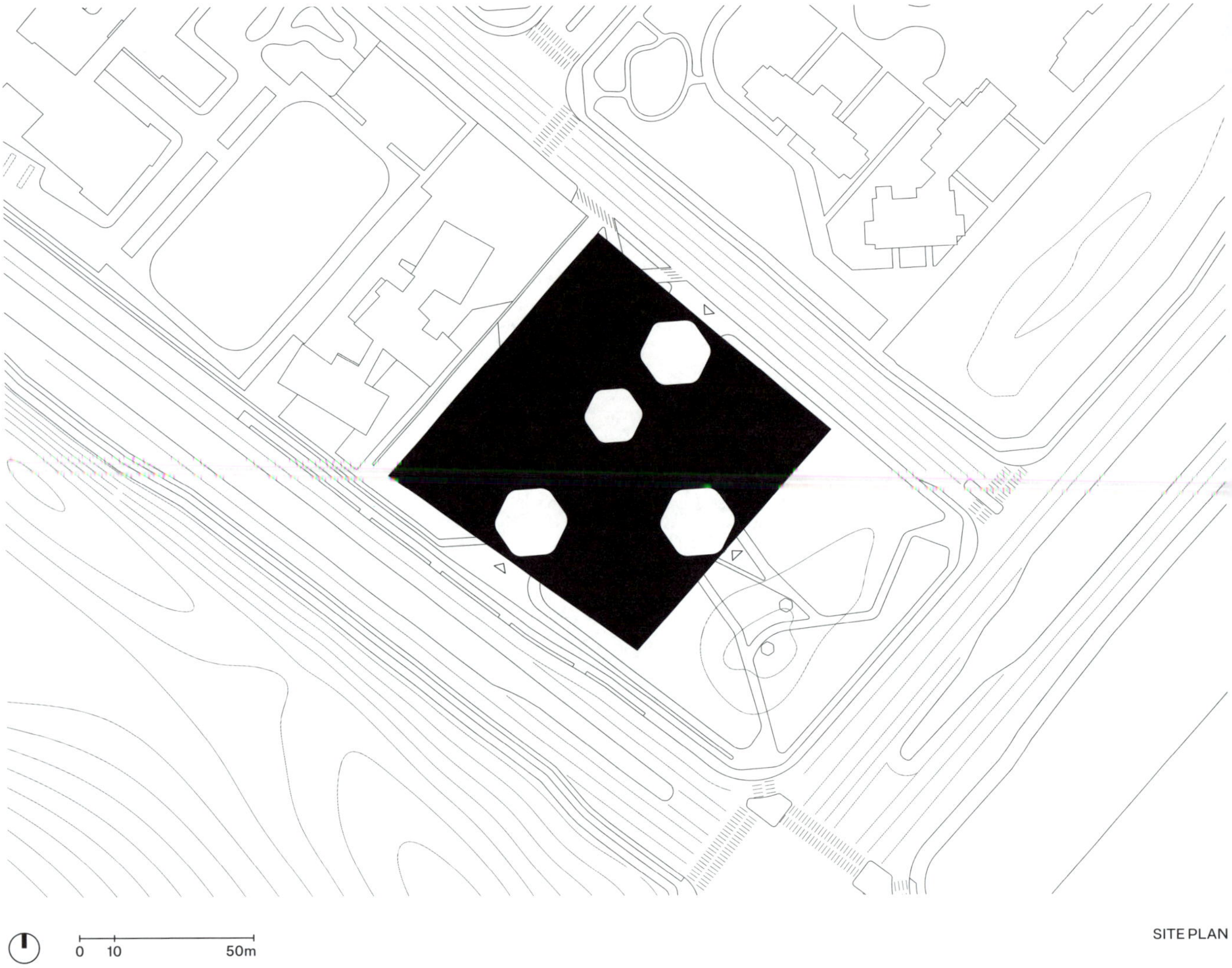


SITE PLAN

Learning Sky proposes a habitat for education and innovation at the heart of Songdo city; a habitat for future learners and a flexible space in which knowledge, making and technology intermingle.

(LS)03
The central zone provides space for flexible study, with views to nature

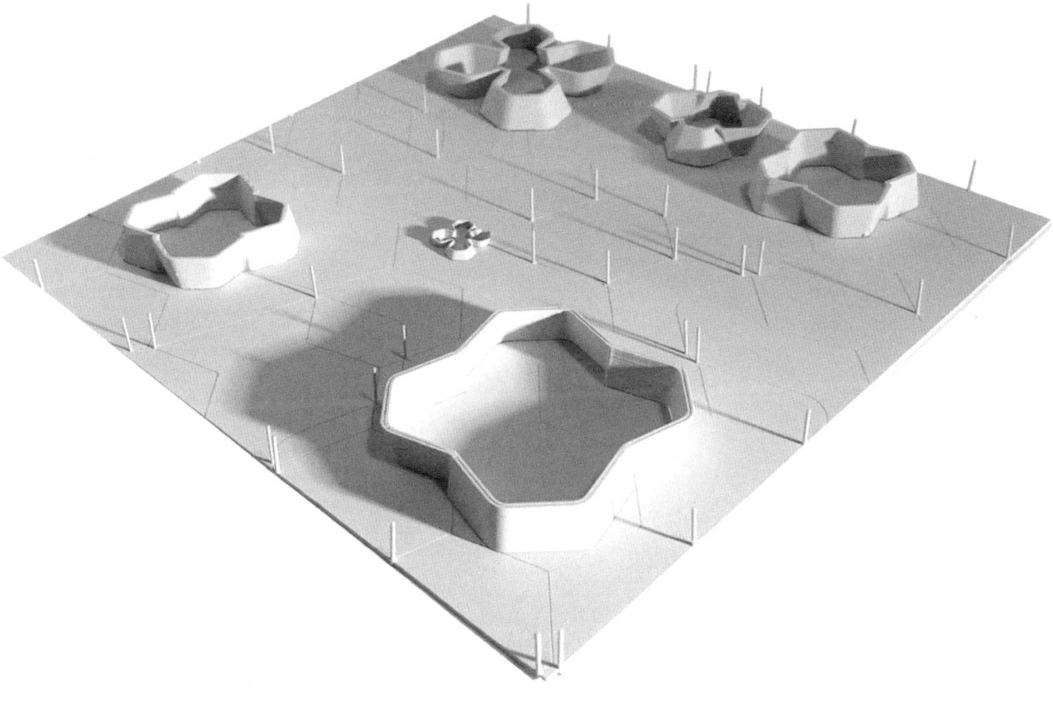

LS)04
The 3D printed structures create cores
hat define closed areas in the building

(LS)05
The low rise building acts as an extension of the landscape, contrasting the urban grain of high rise towers

GROUND FLOOR PLAN

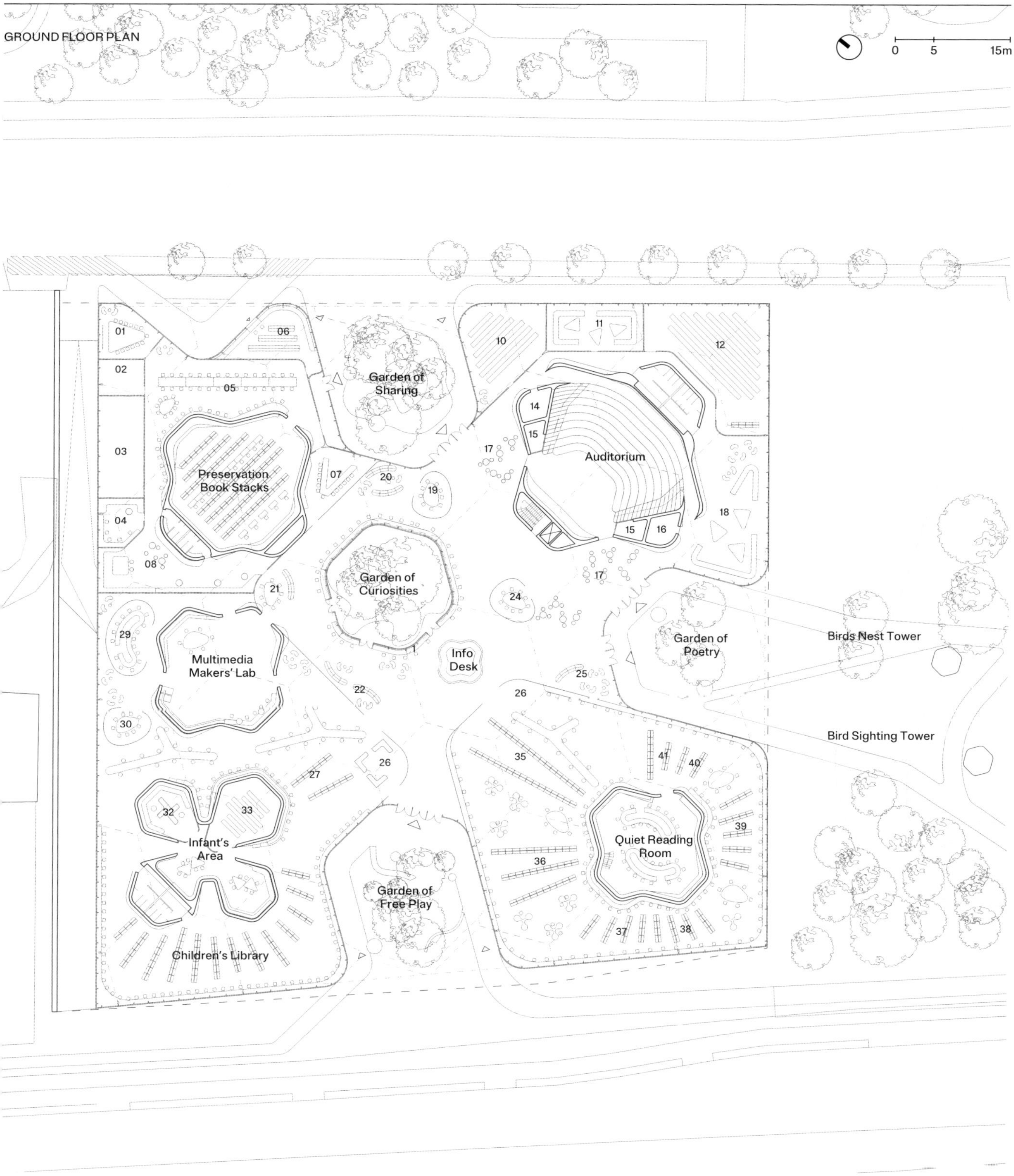


- 01. CONFERENCE ROOM
- 02. ARCHIVE
- 03. SERVER ROOM
- 04. CHIEF OFFICE
- 05. OFFICE
- 06. INCOMING MATERIALS
- 07. VOLUNTEER ROOM
- 08. OFFICE LOUNGE
- 09. LEARNING SPACE
- 10. LEARNING SPACE
- 11. CLUB ROOM
- 12. CULTURAL CLASSROOM
- 13. CULTURAL CLASSROOM
- 14. STORAGE
- 15. TRANSLATION ROOM
- 16. KITCHEN
- 17. BOOK CAFE
- 18. EXHIBITION
- 19. GATHERING STUDIO
- 20. INTERNET CORNER
- 21. COWORKING SPACE
- 22. PERIODICALS
- 23. INFO DESK
- 24. RESEARCH ROOM
- 25. RELAXATION CORNER
- 26. BOOK STATION
- 27. TECHNOLOGY
- 28. TECHNOLOGY
- 29. AUDIO-VISUAL STUDIPO
- 30. VIDEO LAB
- 31. FEEDING ROOM
- 32. FEEDING ROOM
- 33. CLASSROOM
- 34. CLASSROOM
- 35. CULTURE & NON-FICTION
- 36. SCIENCE
- 37. FICTION
- 38. ART & DESIGN
- 39. HISTORY
- 40. TIDAL FLATS / ECOLOGY
- 41. BIRD SIGHTING
- 42. QUIET READING ROOM

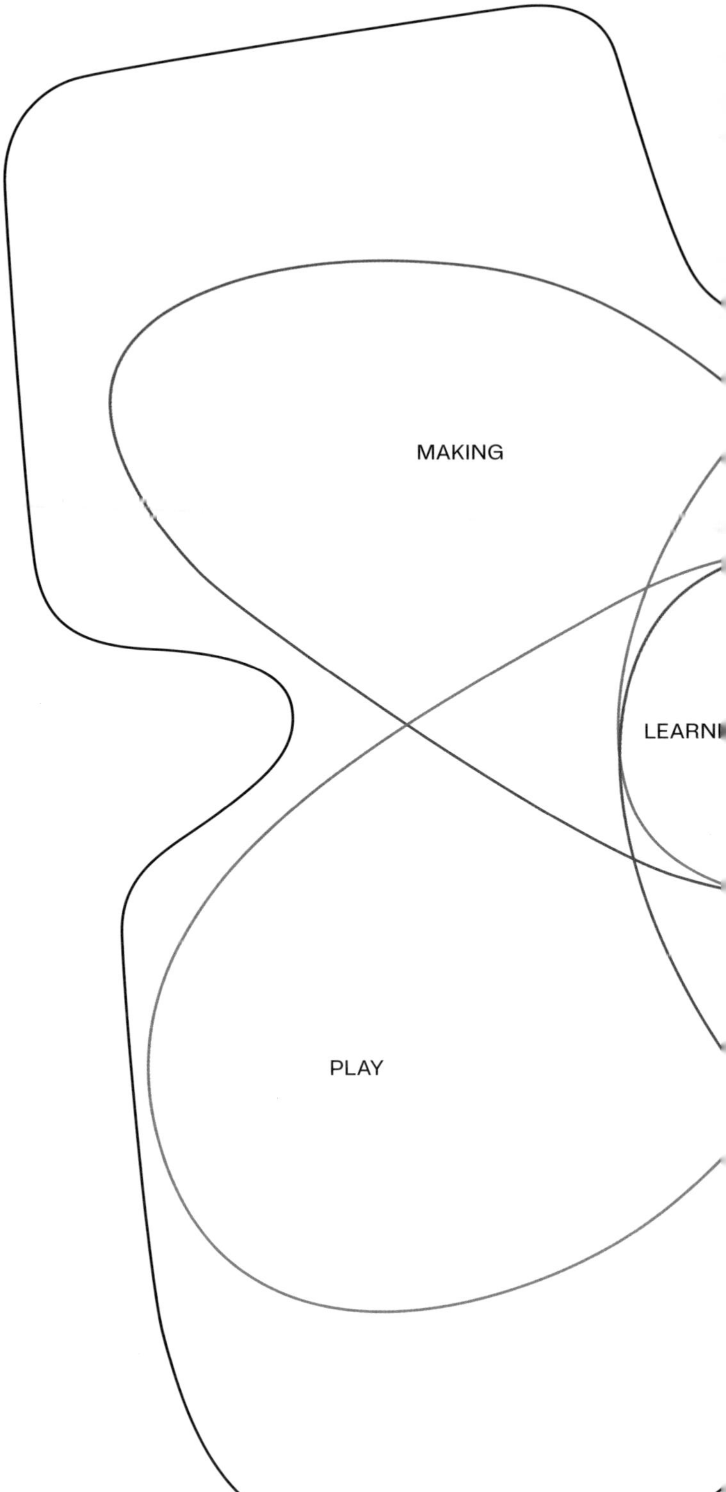
MAKING
LEARNI
PLAY

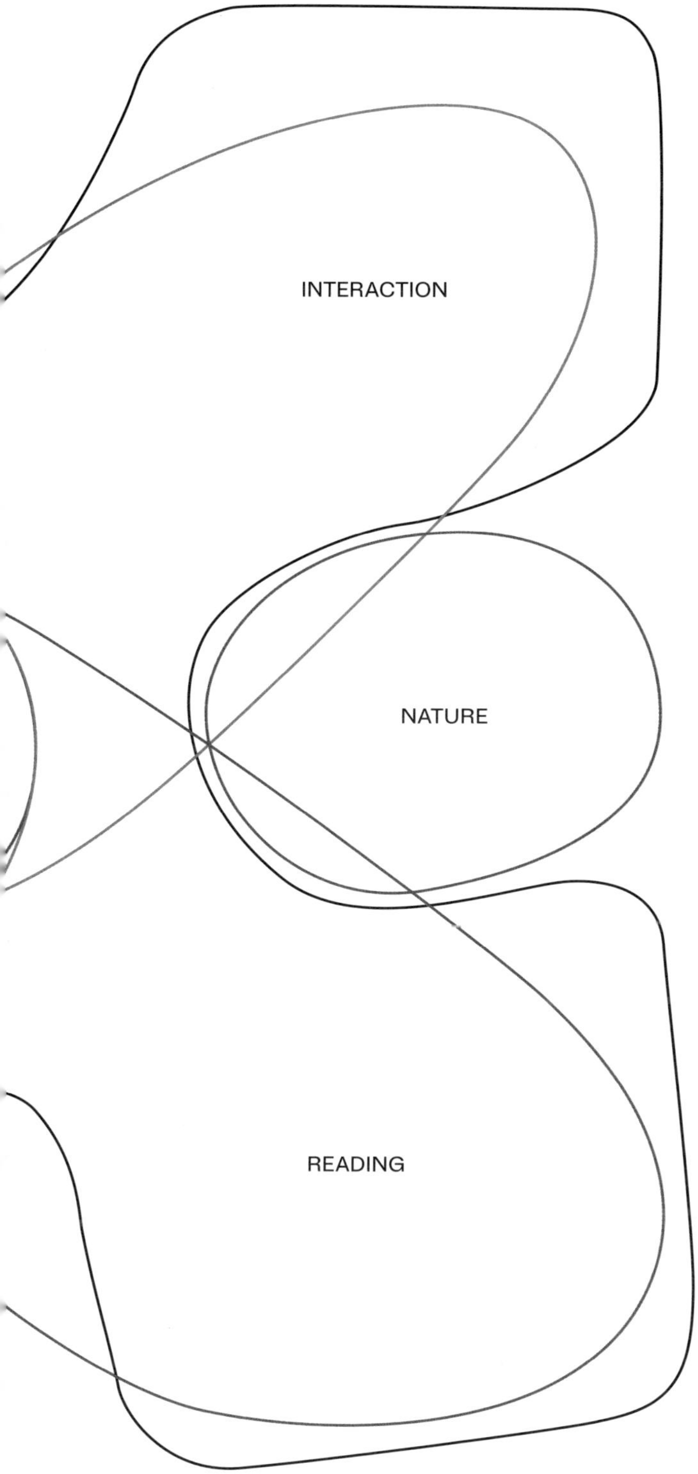
INTERACTION
NATURE
READING

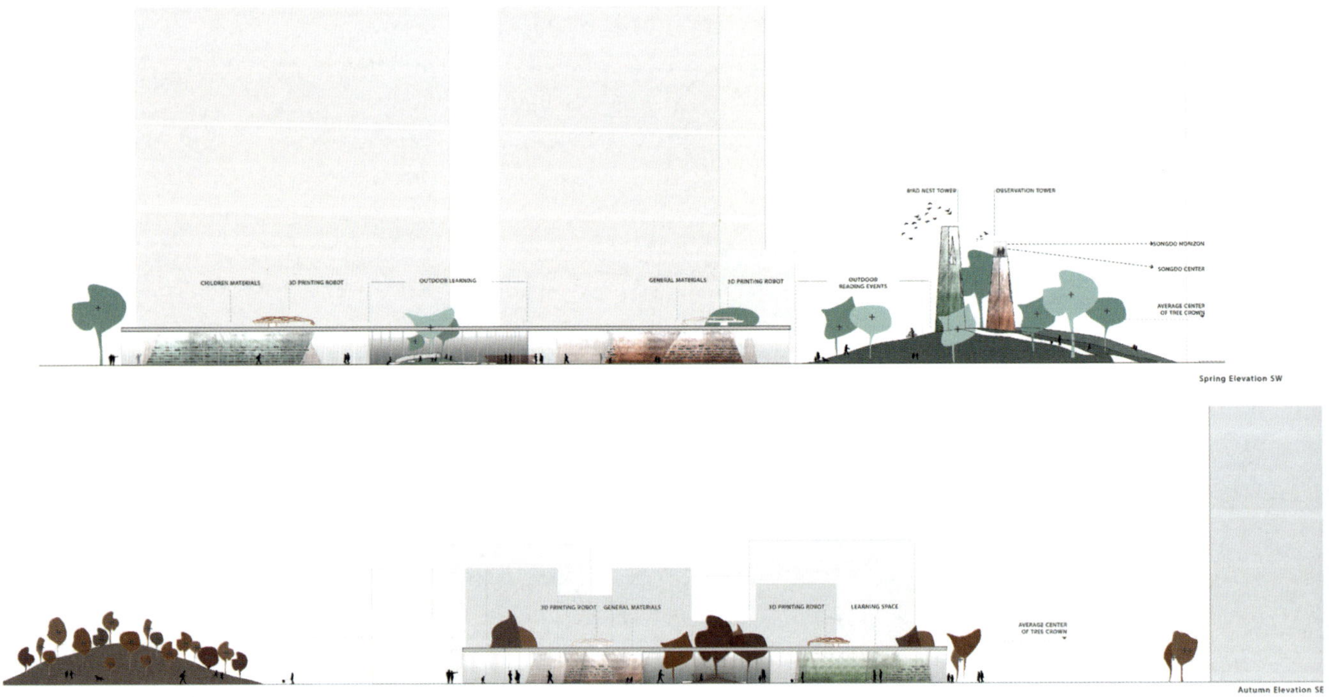


(LS)06
The library colours reflect the changing landscape from spring to autumn

(LS)07

# SELECTIVE PERMEABILI ARCHITECTU

■1 Alfred North Whitehead, Process and Reality. (New York: Free Press, 1978.)
■2 Maurice Merleau-Ponty, Phenomenology of Perception, trans. C. Smith p. 79. (London: Routledge, 2002.)
■3 Bruno Latour, Pandora's Hope: Essays on the Reality of Science Studies. (Cambridge, MA: Harvard University Press, 1999.)
■4 David Ruy, "Returning to (Strange) Objects," tarp: Architecture Manual, issue 10, Spring 2012, pp. 38-4

As Alper Derinboğaz tells us in this book: "We tend to think of things as objects in clearly defined categories, although we live in a tangled web of intertwined connections... This could mean... deeper connections with topography, geology, genetics, ecologies, and natural formations in general." (16) The topic of this book, they add, is "creating spaces in continuity with earth." (16)

IN

E

At first glance this might sound like the exact opposite of the views of object-oriented ontology (OOO). Isn't OOO a theory of objects insofar as they are not in connection with each other, hidden in formalist autonomy from all relations? The question is a misunderstanding. OOO does insist that we consider the autonomous status of entities in their own right, as something separate from all of their connections with other things. This is simply OOO's effort to establish that objects cannot be reduced to the sum total of their effects (or even possible effects) on other objects. This issue is no "straw man," but is found at the heart of some of the most important philosophies of the past century. Alfred North Whitehead says that the most concrete way to understand entities is to grasp them in terms of their "prehensions" (i.e., relations). [1] Maurice-Merleau Ponty claims that "the house itself is not the house seen from nowhere, but the house seen from everywhere," as if a house were merely a sum of views. [2] More recently, Bruno Latour contends that an object (his term is "actor") is nothing more than whatever it modifies, transforms, perturbs, or creates, so that an object is nothing but a totality of actions, which again means a sum of relations. [3] Although the model of the world as a web of holistic interactions might seem liberating at first, David Ruy has stressed the dangers of such an approach for architecture, which might well dissolve into ecological meditations on the carbon footprint if no reasons are given to treat architectural objects as at least partly self-contained. [4]

BY GRAHAM HARMAN

Of course, the opposite claim does not follow. It cannot be the case that OOO demands that objects never relate at all. A quick look at reality is all that is needed to see that some things affect others deeply, that new relations between people or things can result either in extensive benefits or catastrophic degradation. OOO's point is simply that relations cannot be assumed to be effortless or ubiquitous. Some entities can exist in proximity for centuries without influencing each other much or at all, while others need only a fleeting encounter for instant chemistry to occur between them. In architectural terms, although a certain degree of "site-specificity" should help shape ever building, no building ever interacts with all aspects of the site. The architects paves the way for a building to interact with, say, the lighting conditions or historical gravitas of a specific site, while deliberately or accidentally excluding many other relevant aspects of the location.

For this reason, I will speak of the "selective permeability" of buildings, a term borrowed from Matthew Crippen and Vladan Klement. [5] As it happens, Crippen and Klement are heavily inspired by James J. Gibson's notion of "affordances," which one again supports the notion that objects amount to the numerous possible uses they can enable. [6] Now, the authors are fully aware that not all affordances are good: "a cliff-edge affords falling; it looks dangerous and is in fact so to humans... even if one is not currently at risk." But for the most part, they tend to think of affordances as empowering for humans, and as often illegitimately cut off by political power gone awry. Several examples are mentioned from Egypt: probably at the behest of Crippen, who was my department colleague at the American University in Cairo for a number of years. For instance, the authors refer to acts of exclusion or lack of transparency by two former Presidents of the university, as well as the manipulation of Tahrir Square to limit its potential as a revolutionary gathering point in the city. [7] Although these are interesting observations by Crippen and Klement, their own notion of "selective permeability" focuses largely on the contrast between those social groups that are liberated by specific architectural designs and those unable to make proper use of a given building, whether for reasons of political oppression or physical disability. Although they make these points in a spirit of political benevolence, they tend to neglect the inherent architectural need not to make a building permeable by all possible environmental influences. OOO is especially sensitive, however, to the fact that

[5] Matthew Crippen & Vladan Klement, "Architectural Values, Political Affordances, and Selective Permeability," Open Philosophy 3 (2020), pp. 462-477.
[6] James J. Gibson, The Ecological Approach to Visual Perception. Boston: Houghton-Mifflin, 1978.
[7] Crippen & Klement, "Architectural Values, Political Affordances, and Selective Permeability," pp. 466, 467-468.

any object –including the architectural sort– must necessarily restrict its range of references to and interactions with its surroundings. Thus, selective permeability must have a different meaning for the object-oriented thinker from the kind we find in Crippen and Klement.

So, how do we determine those aspects of a building's site or context that are most important for it? The apparently easy answer, as with Latour's notion that actors are to be defined by whatever they modify, transform, perturb, or create, is to look for those aspects of the building and its site that have clear effects on one another. Surprisingly, this method does not work. To say of an object –say, a person or a building– that it is influenced by being in İstanbul sounds like an obligatory truism, but ultimately this tells us very little. For one thing, a building like Alper Derinboğaz's İstanbul City Museum is characterized in large part by its non-affordances with respect to İstanbul: namely, there are all those aspects of the complex city that are completely shut off from the design, which hold back much of İstanbul's wind, much of its ambient noise, as well as the water-pipes and football kicking in the city that is presumably banned from the interior of the museum. Thus, the building becomes a form of "addition by subtraction." And second, even those aspects of the city that are admitted into the museum are not taken simply as they are: rather, the specific quality of İstanbul sunlight is processed by the windows in a specific and highly deliberate way. In short, any direct and transparent relations between İstanbul and the City Museum will be rare; like any building, the museum is defined more by those aspects of the environment that it suppresses or translates. Traditionally, most architectural work is described in terms of its "form" and its "function," even in those cases where architects deny the existence of one of these terms, or instead denies any strict distinction between the two. OOO is skeptical toward such efforts, and worries about another difficulty instead. Namely, the "function" of a building is too often considered in terms of its explicit affordances or program, thereby dissolving it into its relations. If architecture only needed to be transparently serviceable, then good engineering would suffice, and no design would be necessary. And furthermore, the "form" of a building is also usually exhausted by its appearance to a human viewer, which is impossible for several reasons– one of which is that a building can be experienced from multiple locations both outside and inside the building, so that no specific visual appearance will ever be equivalent to its form. If architecture were equivalent to appearance, its temporal character would be missed, and it might as well be replaced by a painting, or at least a sculpture.

From these considerations, we can see that architecture must not be reduced to relational terms. Functionally speaking, a building certainly exists in relation to its site and its purpose. But for it to be architecture, there needs to be a much looser relation between a building and its function, as can be seen from the fact that many buildings are flexible enough to serve multiple purposes during their lifetime. In this spirit, Aldo Rossi offers examples of "important urban artifacts whose function has changed over time or for which a specific function does not even exist." [8] As for form, it should also be separated by a gap from any specific human visual experience of the form. This can be done by emphasizing the ways in which architectural form is often partly concealed from the spectator, which is of course a classic OOO theme. But perhaps more important is the fact that architectural form is experienced temporally through a series of wanderings on the outside and inside of any edifice. This reminds us that form in architecture is never instantaneous, and must be held together in memory. But it also raises another crucial object-oriented concern: the fact that the form of a building involves a sequence between different parts of the architectural object, which makes us think about the way that architectural components relate to each other. Insofar as object-object relations are almost entirely excluded from post-Kantian philosophy, this is one of those weighty topics where architecture can take the lead over philosophy rather than the reverse.

[8] Aldo Rossi, Architecture of the City, trans. D. Ghiardo & J. Ockman, p. 346. (Cambridge, MA: MIT Pressm 1984.)

(G)03

(G)04

# PROJECT CREDITS

MODALITIES OF THE SPONTANEOUS
(MS)

VILLA TOPOS
(VT)

| | |
|---|---|
| EXHIBITOR | ALPER DERİNBOĞAZ |
| RESEARCH TEAM | AHMET ÜNVEREN, ZOE GEORGOU |
| EDITORS | ÖMER KANIPAK, ENİSE BURCU DERİNBOĞAZ |
| CURATOR | REM KOOLHAAS |
| COORDINATOR | PELİN DERVİŞ |
| PAVILION CURATOR | MURAT TABANLIOĞLU |
| PHOTOGRAPHY | ITALO RONDINELLA |

| | |
|---|---|
| ARCHITECT | ALPER DERİNBOĞAZ |
| PROJECT TEAM | EGEMEN ONUR KAYA, ŞEVKİ TOPÇU, REYYAN ÇULCU, DORUK KAYALI, ÖMER MANAV |
| STRUCTURAL DESIGN | İNTAÇ ENGINEERING |
| CONSTRUCTION | MKCONSTRCUTION |

OBLIQUE LAND
(OL)

SCIENCE ISLAND
(SI)

| | |
|---|---|
| ARCHITECT | ALPER DERİNBOĞAZ |
| COLLABORATORS | DOT THEATRE / ZORLU PSM |
| DIRECTOR | MURAT DALTABAN |
| STRUCTURAL DESIGNER | ALFA ÇELİK, BALKAR ENGINEERING |
| LIGHTING DESIGN | CEM YILMAZER |
| PROJECT TEAM | EGEMEN ONUR KAYA |

| | |
|---|---|
| ARCHIECT | ALPER DERİNBOĞAZ |
| SUSTAINABILITY STRATEGY | TRANSSOLAR |
| PROJECT TEAM | ŞEVKİ TOPÇU, THIBAULT JALBY, ECEM ÇINAR, CANSU ALTINTAŞ, SEDA DURAN, AYGÜL ÇINAR, DENİZ KARADERE, ALİ ASAD, MAŽVYDAS SAMUOLIS |
| VISUALS | POLYNATES |

KUORI
(K)

ECOTONE
(E)

| | |
|---|---|
| ARCHITECT | ALPER DERİNBOĞAZ |
| PROJECT TEAM | RANA IRMAK AKSOY, EGEMEN ONUR KAYA, EMMY BACHARACH, PINAR KÖMÜRCÜ, EKİN CEM TÜMBEK, EZGİ IŞIK, PAULINA SAWCZUK |
| LANDSCAPE DESIGN | ENİSE BURCU DERİNBOĞAZ, İZEL BEŞİKÇİ |
| PLANNING CONSULTANT | HÜSEYİN KAHVECİOĞLU |
| HISTORY & PRESERVATION | KUTAY KARABAĞ |
| SUSTAINABILITY STRATEGY | SELÇUK AVCI |
| LOCAL CONSULTANT | HÜSEYİN YANAR |
| SUSTAINABLE SERVICING | HENRY LUKER |
| LIGHTING DESIGN | JARI VUORINEN |

| | |
|---|---|
| ARCHIECT | ALPER DERİNBOĞAZ |
| PROJECT TEAM | EGEMEN ONUR KAYA, EKİN CEM TÜMBEK, PINAR KÖMÜRCÜ, EMMY BACHARACH, BERKAY YÜCEBAŞ, TOLGA HALİL AKŞAHİN, CANSU GÖSTERİŞLİ, HAN SEKİ |
| CONSULTANTS | |
| STRUCTURAL PEER REVIEW | PROF. PETER BAUER, WERKRAUM |
| STRUCTURAL ENGINEERING | PARLAR ENGINEERING |
| SUSTAINABILITY CONSULTANT | DR. PINAR SİPAHİ |
| MECHANICAL ENGINEERING | ÇİLİNGİROĞLU ENGINEERING |
| ELECTRICAL ENGINEERING | SANAYİ ENGINEERING |

PANORAMA
(P)

FİTAŞ PASSAGE
(FP)

| | |
|---|---|
| ARCHITECT | ALPER DERİNBOĞAZ IN COLLABORATION WITH ANDREAS FOGARASI |
| COMMISSION | THE BRITISH COUNCIL |
| COORDINATOR | ESRA SARIGEDİK |

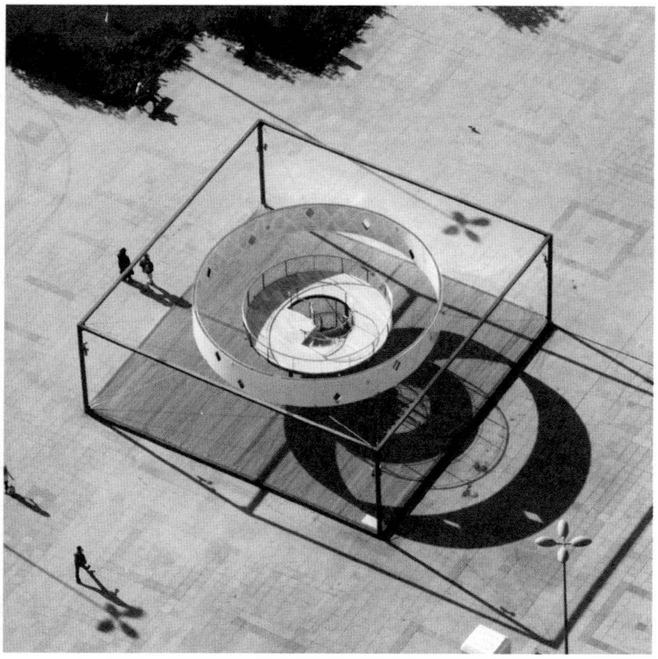

| | |
|---|---|
| ARCHITECT | ALPER DERİNBOĞAZ IN COLLABORATION WITH YETKİN BAŞARIR |
| PROJECT TEAM | EGEMEN ONUR KAYA, DORUK KAYALI |
| GRAPHIC DESIGN | YETKİN BAŞARIR |
| CONSTRUCTION | NOVA |

MUSEUM OF İSTANBUL
(Mİ)

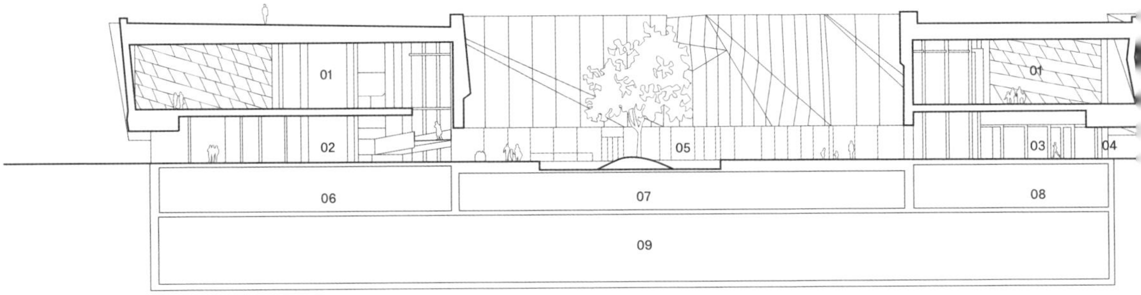

| | |
|---|---|
| ARCHITECT | ALPER DERİNBOĞAZ |
| PROJECT TEAM | CANSU ALTINTAŞ, EGEMEN ONUR KAYA, THIBAULT JALBY, SİNAN AZİZAĞAOĞLU, MERYEM ÇAVUŞLAR, ŞEVKİ TOPÇU, ECEM ÇINAR, ORÇUN GİRGİN |
| CONSULTANTS | |
| CURATORIAL DESIGN | LUCA MOLINARI, ANJA VISINI |
| COMPUTATIONAL CONSULTANCY | SATORU SUGIHARA |
| STRUCTURAL ENGINEERING | PETER BAUER, WERKRAUM INGENIEURE 8 BALKAR CONSTRUCTION |
| EARTHQUAKE ENGINEERING | NURAY AYDINOĞLU, ERKAN ÖZER |
| FAÇADE ENGINEERING | ANDY WATTS, NEWTECNIC |
| LANDSCAPE DESIGN | PRAXIS LANDSCAPE |
| ELECTRICAL ENGINEERING | HB TEKNİK |
| MECHANICAL ENGINEERING | ÇİLİNGİROĞLU ENGINEERING |
| BIM CONSULTANCY | LATERNA PARTNERS |
| LIGHTING DESIGN | SLD STUDIO |
| ORIENTATION DESIGN | POMPAA DESIGN |
| GEOTECHNICAL | BİLGİ 2000 |
| FIRE ENGINEERING | ISTANBUL TECHNICAL UNIVERSITY |
| INFRASTRUCTURE ENGINEERING | ERIMCO |
| SUSTAINABILITY CONSULTANT | ERKE |
| PROJECT MANAGEMENT | PY INTERNATIONAL CONSULTANCY |
| ACADEMIC CONSULTANTS | PROF. DR. ENGİN AKYÜREK (KOÇ UNIVERSITY), PROF. DR. UFUK KOCABAŞ (ISTANBUL UNIVERSITY), PROF. DR. MEHMET ÖZDOGAN (ISTANBUL UNIVERSITY), PROF. DR. BAHA TANMAN (ISTANBUL UNIVERSITY), PROF. DR. VEDAT ONAR (ISTANBUL UNIVERSITY), PROF. DR. OĞUZ TEKİN (ISTANBUL UNIVERSITY), PROF. DR. HÜLYA TEZCAN, PROF. DR. ATİLLA YÜCEL, PROF. DR. ARZU ERDEM (KADIR HAS UNIVERSITY), PROF. DR. ASLIHAN ŞENEL (ISTANBUL TECHNICAL UNIVERSITY), ARZU HAKSUN GÜVENILIR (MİMAR SİNAN UNIVERSITY) |

AUGMENTED STRUCTURES
(AS)

LEARNING SKY
(LS)

ARCHITECT ALPER DERİNBOĞAZ IN COLLABORATION WITH REFİK ANADOL

PROJECT TEAM MAURIZIO BRAGGIOTTI, YAVUZ SELİM CAN, CANAN ÇENGEL, ŞENER ÇARDAK, CEYHUN DERİNBOĞAZ, FREDERIK DE SMEDT, KORKUT ERDUR, EFSUN ERKILIÇ, MELİS EYÜBOĞLU, AYBER GÜLFER, EFE MERT KAYA, MEHMET KOCAOĞLU, CİHANER NİŞANCI, OZAN ÖZDILEK, YELIZ ÖZSOY, ÇAĞLAR ÖZTÜRK, BÜLENT TUNÇAY, VEYSEL UĞURLU, İDİL SEREN YÜCEL, MUSTAFA ERCAN ZIRH

PHOTOGRAPHY MAURIZIO BRAGGIOTTI

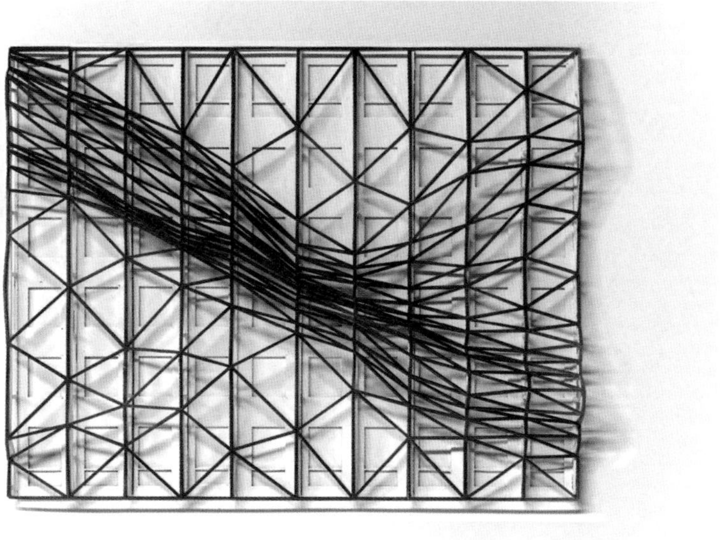

ARCHITECT ALPER DERİNBOĞAZ

LIBRARY CONSULTANT DR. JAMES W. P. CAMPBELL

PARAMETRIC DESIGN SATORU SUGIHARA, LEVENT OZRUH

PROJECT TEAM ECE EMANETOĞLU, YUSUF ARAS KALKAN, PINAR KOMÜRCÜ, EMMY BACHARACH, EGEMEN KAYA, NİDA DILARA KARIŞIK, NAZLIM DEMİR, SENA KARATOPRAK, DENİZ KARADERE, MEHMET ALİ AZCAN

LANDSCAPE DESIGN PRAXIS LANDSCAPE

# SPECIAL THANKS TO OUR SUPPORTERS:

# PHOTO CREDITS

GEOSPACES
(G)01 CLAUDIA BADEA
(G)02 EMMY BACHARACH
EARTH SHAPES
(ES)01
(MS)01 ITALO RONDINELLA
(MS)02 ANDREA AVEZZU
(MS)03
(MS)04
(MS)05
(MS)06
(VT)01 CEMAL EMDEN
(VT)02 SERRA DURAN
(VT)03 SERRA DURAN
(VT)04 CEMAL EMDEN
(VT)05
(VT)06
(VT)07
(VT)08 CEMAL EMDEN
(VT)09
(VT)10
(VT)11
(OL)01
(OL)02 EMRE GÖKMENOĞLU
(OL)03
(OL)04
ITERATIONS
(I)01
(I)02 RANDOLPH FEMMER
(I)03
(I)04
(SI)01
(SI)02
(SI)03
(SI)04
(SI)05
(SI)06
(SI)07
(K)01
(K)02
(K)03
(K)04
(K)05
(K)06
(K)07
TRANSITIONS
(T)01
(T)02
(E)01
(E)02
(P)01 BÜŞRA YELTEKİN
(P)02 ANDREAS FOGARASI
(P)03 BRITISH COUNCIL ISTANBUL
(P)04 BÜŞRA YELTEKİN
(P)05
EVOLUTIONS
(E)01
(E)02 CANER CANGÜL

| | |
|---|---|
| (FP)01 | ORHAN KOLUKISA |
| (FP)02 | |
| (FP)03 | |
| (FP)04 | ORHAN KOLUKISA |
| (FP)05 | CEMAL EMDEN |
| (FP)06 | ORHAN KOLUKISA |
| (Mİ)01 | |
| (Mİ)02 | BÜŞRA YELTEKİN |
| (Mİ)03 | BÜŞRA YELTEKİN |
| (Mİ)04 | ORHAN KOLUKISA |
| (Mİ)05 | |
| (Mİ)06 | ORHAN KOLUKISA |
| FUTURE HYBRIDITY | |
| (FH)01 | |
| (FH)02 | FROM "LE CORBUSIER, OEUVRE COMPLÈTE 1938-46" |
| (AS)01 | ORHAN KOLUKISA |
| (AS)02 | |
| (AS)03 | |
| (AS)04 | |
| (LS)01 | |
| (LS)01 | |
| (LS)01 | |
| (LS)01 | |
| (LS)01 | |
| (LS)01 | |
| (LS)01 | |

# ALPER DERİNBO

# BIOGRAPHY

ALPER DERİNBOĞAZ is an architect and academic seeking communal relationships between environment and spatial elements through scientific strategies. His experiments vary from installations to large-scale cultural institutions, including the new İstanbul City Museum nearing compilation. Derinboğaz leads one of "the best young architecture practices" Salon as listed by ArchDaily besides his studio in ITU.

AZ

He studied at UCLA (Fulbright), where he had the Graduate Award. His research has been exhibited in biennales and museums including the first İstanbul Design Biennale. He exhibited at the Koolhaas-curated Venice Architecture Biennale in 2014 with his work Modalities of the Spontaneous (MS), an in-depth study of urbanization in relationship with geography, at the national chapter. His projects have won awards in international competitions from Songdo Library to Kaunas Science Island. His work has been featured in renowned media including Time, Dezeen and Frame. He was selected as one of the 40 top young architects in Europe in 2019, and in Archdaily's Best Young Practices in 2020. He has been gathering his research under the umbrella of 'Geospaces' since 2011.

ACADEMIC BACKGROUND

2007-2008 M.A. ARCHITECTURE II SECOND PROFESSIONAL DEGREE, UNIVERSITY OF CALIFORNIA, LOS ANGELES

2000-2005 B.A. ARCHITECTURE, MAGNA CUM LAUDE, ISTANBUL TECHNICAL UNIVERSITY

RECOGNITIONS

2020 ARCHDAILY BEST YOUNG PRACTICES AWARD

2019 EUROPE 40 UNDER 40 THE EUROPEAN ARCHITECTURE CENTER

2011 YOUNG ARCHITECT OF THE YEAR AWARD BY ARKITERA

2008 UCLA SCHOOL OF ARCHITECTURE GRADUATE AWARD

2008 FULBRIGHT PROGRAM

2005 TURKEY ARCHITECTURE ASSOCIATION SUCCESS AWARD

SELECTED AWARDS

2021 MEMORIAL DESIGN FOR PANDEMICS AND HEALTH LABOURERS COMPETITION, SECOND PRIZE

2021 SONGDO LIBRARY INTERNATIONAL DESIGN COMPETITION, HONORABLE MENTION

2020 İSTANBUL'S CEMETERY DESIGN COMPETITION (CIHAT BURAK) 1ST PRIZE

2020 MELES STREAM AS ECOLOGICAL CORRIDOR URBAN DESIGN COMPETITION, WINNER OF 1ST PRIZE

2020 GOLDEN HORN WATERFRONT DESIGN COMPETITION, 1ST MENTION

2020 VELUX BRINGING LIGHT TO LIFE AWARD, CHINIMACHIN MUSEUM

2019 YOUNG ARCHITECTS SELECTION & EXHIBITION, THE CIRCLE

2018 GREEN GOOD DESIGN AWARDS, WINNER, CHICAGO ATHENAEUM (ANTALYA GREENHUB MASTERPLAN)

2017 GERMAN DESIGN AWARDS, WINNER, GERMAN DESIGN COUNCIL (PARKOPERA)

2016 INTERNATIONAL CONTEST FOR THE NEW NATIONAL SCIENCE AND INNOVATION CENTER HONORABLE MENTION

| | |
|---|---|
| 2016 | 2A ASIA AWARDS FINALIST (ANTALYA GREENHUB MASTERPLAN, PARKOPERA) |
| 2016 | WORLD ARCHITECTURE AWARDS WINNER (OFFICE CENTRAL) |
| 2016 | WAF FINALIST (PARKOPERA) |
| 2016 | THE PLAN AWARDS FINALIST (ANTALYA GREENHUB MASTERPLAN) |
| 2016 | VALLEY OF LIFE INTERNATIONAL COMPETITION, 3TH PRIZE |
| 2015 | INTERNATIONAL ARCHITIZER A+ AWARD SPECIAL MENTION |
| 2015 | PARKOPERA, NATIONAL COMPETITION WINNER OF 1ST MENTION |
| 2015 | BEYLİKDÜZÜ VALLEY AND BRIDGE NATIONAL COMPETITION WINNER OF MENTION |
| 2011 | BEST BUILDINGS OF 2011 BY ARKIV (AUGMENTED STRUCTRES, GATE, PANAROMA) |
| 2006 | SMD "S.O.S. İSTANBUL SEASHORES RENEWAL COMPETITION", 1ST PRIZE |
| 2005 | INTERNATIONAL EUROPAN8 "RENEWAL FOR WHICH INHABITANTS?", ANTALYA KEPEZ (TU) |
| 2004 | UIA "CELEBRATING CITIES INTERNATIONAL COMPETITION", JURY GREAT PRIZE |

## JURY MEMBERSHIPS

| | |
|---|---|
| 2021.04 | FUTURATE SPACE CREATIVE BUSINESS CUP İSTANBUL |
| 2020.06 | ARCHASM 'HOME: DESIGN YOUR DREAM' COMPETITION |
| 2020.01 | SKYSCRAPER COMPETITION, EVOLO MAGAZINE |
| 2019.06 | 24H COMPETITION 30TH EDITION, MOZAMBIQUE |
| 2019.05 | SCHOOL OF ARCHITECTURE - ÇUHADAROĞLU COMPETITION |
| 2019.05 | LIVING PAMUKKALE COMPETITION |
| 2016.05 | NATIONAL ARCHITECTURE STUDENTS COMPETITION |
| 2016.03 | NOAH'S ARK INTERNATIONAL COMPETITION IDEAS |
| 2015.05 | AWR NYC SKY CONDO NEW YORK CITY FARM TOWER COMPETITION |
| 2013.01 | BORUSAN KINDERGARTEN COMPETITION |

## STUDIOS

| | |
|---|---|
| 2020.09 | ARCH402-HAYDARPAŞA SILOS, ISTANBUL TECHNICAL UNIVERSITY |
| 2019.09 | BIODESIGN INSTITUTE A VENUE FOR SCIENCE AND COMMUNITY, GRADUATION JURY, ISTANBUL TECHNICAL UNIVERSITY |
| 2018.09 | ECOLOGIES OF LIVING SPECULATIONS FOR HOUSING +, GRADUATION JURY, ISTANBUL TECHNICAL UNIVERSITY |
| 2018.12 | GRADUATION JURY, ISTANBUL BILGI UNIVERSITY |
| 2017.08 | LINK EXPERIMENTS ON NATURE, ARCHITECTURE & PRODUCTION MESH, ARCHITECTURAL DESIGN V, ISTANBUL TECHNICAL UNIVERSITY |
| 2017.02 | LOG THE NEW MEDIA MUSEUM & A LOCAL ARCHIVE, ARCHITETURAL DESIGN VI, ISTANBUL TECHNICAL UNIVESITY |
| 2016.08 | COLLECTIVE DWELLING, ARCHITECTURAL DESIGN VI, ISTANBUL TECHNICAL UNIVERSITY |
| 2016.02 | FORM OF DOING COMMUNITY SPACES IN THE CITY |

## EXHIBITIONS

| | |
|---|---|
| 2022 | "GEOSPACES", MILANO DESIGN WEEK, ARENA GALLERY, MILAN, ITALY |
| 2022 | "COMMONS & COMMUNITIES GLOBAL ARCHITECTURAL EXHIBITION", DANISH CULTURAL INSTITUTE |
| 2014 | "MODALITIES OF THE SPONTANEOUS", PAVILION OF TURKEY AT LA BIENNALE DI VENEZIA, VENICE |
| 2017 | "CONDENSE", SOUL OF CITY EXHIBITION, MARMOMACC VERONA, ITALY |
| 2021 | "GEOSPACES: CITY AS NEW NATURE", READING ROOM INSTALLATION, ROYAL ACADEMY OF SPAIN, ROME |
| 2015 | "KEPEZ ANTALYA", MIPIM, CANNES, FRANCE |
| 2020 | "TRANSIENT / FANI" AT 'SCALE' EXHIBITION, VERSUS ART PROJECT |
| 2018 | "SPACE GRAPH_" EXHIBITION, VERSUS ART PROJECT |
| 2017 | "RESET-FOIL", FUTURE TELLERS EXHIBITION, DIGILOGUE |
| 2017 | "FREQUENCY", HELIX EXHIBITION, YAPI KREDİ CULTURE AND ART, ISTANBUL |
| 2016 | "PASSAGE-SPATIAL SIMULATION", WAVES |
| 2016 | "GREENHUB ANTALYA", MIPIM, CANNES, FRANCE |
| 2014 | VÇMD DREAMS TO REALITIES EXHIBITION, COLLECTIVE SCHOOL, İSTANBUL |

| | |
|---|---|
| 2013 | INTERNATIONAL ANTALYA BIENNIAL |
| 2012 | "AUGMENTED STRUCTURES V2.0, ISTANBUL DESIGN BIENNIAL |
| 2011 | "AUGMENTED STRUCTURES V1.0, YAPI KREDI CULTURE AND ART CENTER |
| 2010 | "GIRFT", ISTANBUL BILGI UNIVERSITY |
| 2007 | "FLOATED", ELEFSINA, GREECE |
| 2006 | "TRASHED", COMMON PLACE, BUDAPEST, HUNGARY |
| 2006 | "SAUNA" LETTERFRACK, IRELAND |
| 2005 | "VIDEOMASS", BERGÜN, SWITZERLAND |
| 2004 | "TOUCHED", LILLE, FRANCE |

LECTURES

| | |
|---|---|
| 2022 | SHARE SOFIA FORUM, KEYNOTE SPEAKER |
| 2022 | DAAILY BAR AT SWISS CORNER, MILAN |
| 2022 | GEOSPACES OPEN LECTURE, BERLIN INTERNATIONAL |
| 2021 | ARTS & ECOLOGY PANEL, SÓNAR+D ISTANBUL, PANELIST |
| 2021 | FULBRIGHT ALUMNI ASSOCIATION, DISTINGUISHED GUEST SPEAKER |
| 2020 | "SPATIAL ECOLOGIES", KHAS |
| 2019 | "OPEN BOUNDARY", LONDON FESTIVAL OF ARCHITECTURE 2019, LONDON |
| 2019 | "INNOVATION FOR CITIES", ARCH AND DESIGN SUMMIT 2019 |
| 2017 | "CODES OF ARCHITECTURE", INTERNATIONAL ARCHITECTURE AND DESIGN SYMPOSIUM |
| 2017 | "DESIGN ENCOUNTERS", MEF UNIVERSITY |
| 2016 | "E-DIMENSION, KEYNOTE" SPEECH, EKO DESIGN CONFERENCE |
| 2015 | "CITY URGENCIES" NEW GENERATION FESTIVAL, GENOVA |
| 2015 | "BEAUTY, UGLY AND THE CITY" SOHO HOUSE |
| 2015 | "PERFORMATIVITY AND GRADIENTS IN DESIGN" BILGI UNIVERSITY |
| 2015 | "MODALITIES OF SPONTANEOUS" BAHCESEHIR UNIVERSITY |
| 2014 | "DESIGN ECOLOGIES", NEW GENERATIONS, FLORENCE |
| 2014 | "DIRTY ROTTEN BEAUTY", ARKIMEET |
| 2014 | "SCALE OPERATIONS", LEBANESE AMERICAN UNIVERSITY, BEIRUT |
| 2014 | "INTRICATE TERRITORIES" POLIS UNIVERSITY, TIRANA, ALBANIA |
| 2013 | "PUBLIC ART AND ARCHITECTURAL LUNAPARKS" ARCHITECTURAL ASSOCIATION PUBLIC BITS |
| 2009 | "REPOSE", SUPERM.ARCH.ET, DARFO, ITALY |

2020 COVID
2020 ECOTONE
2019 OBLIQUE LAND
2019 FİTAŞ PASSAGE
2018
2017
2016 SCIENCE ISLAND (KAUNAS)
2015 İSTANBUL CITY MUSEUM
2014
2013
2012
2011 AUGMENTED STRUCTURES DIGITAL MAPPING (İSTANBUL)
2010
2009
2008
2007

# TIMELINE

2006
2005
2004
2003
2002
2001
2000
1999 MARMARA EARTHQUAKE
1998
1997
1996
1995 EARTH MOVES BY BERNARD CACHE
SUSTAINABILITY DEVELOPMENT
(* ARCHITECTURE IS RESPONSIBLE %40 CARBON EMISSION)
1994
1993
1992
1991
1990
1989 BERLIN WALL FELL
1988
1987
1986

# IN RELATION

1985
1984
1983
1982
1981
1980
1979
1978
1977
1976
1975
1974 LEFEBVRE PRODUCTION OF SPACE
1973
1972
1971
1970
1969 SUPERSTUDIO
(THE CONTINUOUS MONUMENT)
1968 APOLLO 8
(CHANGES OUR PERCEPTION OF THE SCALE OF EARTH)

1963 CLAUDE PARENT

(THE OBLIQUE FUNCTION WAS FIRST DEVELOPED)

1962
1961
1960
1959
1958
1957

# TO EARTH

1956
1955
1954
1953
1952 ALAN TURING'S MORPHOGENESIS
1951
1950
1949
1948
1947
1946
1945
1944
1943
1942
1941
1940
1939 MUSEUM OF UNLIMITED GROWTH (LE CORBUSIER)
1938
1937
1936
1935
1934
1933
1932
1930
1929 VILLA SAVOYE (LE CORBUSIER)
1928
1927
1926
1925
1924
1923
1922
1921
1920
1919 VOYAGE D'ORIENT (LE CORBUSIER)
918-1756
755 PRIMITIVE HUT: LAUGIER'S THEORY ABOUT THE ROOTS OF ARCHITECTURE
754-1647
646 SAN CARLINO CHURCH ALLE QUATTRO FONTANE
645-1506
505 DEL BELVEDERE
3C
85 BC BYZANTIUM FIRST CITY WALLS BUILT
3000-2000 BC STONEHENGE
5000 BC WHEEL INVENTED, MESOPOTAMIA
710 BC ÇATALHÖYÜK (PROTO CITY SETTLEMENT IN SOUTHERN ANATOLIA)
2,000 YEARS AGO CAVES INHABITED IN HASANKEYF, MESOPOTAMIA
00,00 YEARS AGO NEANDERTHAL HUMANS DWELT IN CAVES IN EUROPE AND WESTERN ASIA
MILLION YEARS AGO FIRE FIRST USED TO PRODUCE HEAT FROM BIOMASS

DISTRIBUTION
ACTAR D, INC. NEW YORK, BARCELONA.

NEW YORK
440 PARK AVENUE SOUTH, 17TH FLOOR
NEW YORK, NY 10016, USA
T +1 2129662207
salesnewyork@actar-d.com

BARCELONA
ROCA I BATLLE 2
08023 BARCELONA, SPAIN
T +34 933 282 183
eurosales@actar-d.com

INDEXING
ENGLISH ISBN: 978-1-63840-053-0
LIBRARY OF CONGRESS CONTROL NUMBER: 2022943617

PUBLICATION DATE
JANUARY 2023

FIRST EDITION

PRINTED IN İSTANBUL, TURKEY, JANUARY 2023